MONEY SMARTS

THE GUIDE TO

SAVING MONEY

325 VALUABLE TIPS THAT WILL HELP YOU S·T·R·E·T·C·H YOUR DOLLARS

Other Money Smarts titles from the Globe Pequot Press
by David L. Scott

The Guide to Personal Budgeting
The Guide to Investing in Common Stocks
The Guide to Investing in Bonds
The Guide to Investing in Mutual Funds
The Guide to Buying Insurance
The Guide to Managing Credit
The Guide to Tax-Saving Investing
The Guide to Investing for Current Income

Also by David L. Scott

Dictionary of Accounting
Fundamentals of the Time Value of Money
How Wall Street Works: The Basics and Beyond
Investing in Tax-Saving Municipal Bonds
The Investor's Guide to Discount Brokers
Municipal Bonds: The Basics and Beyond
Security Investments
Understanding and Managing Investment Risk and Return
Wall Street Words

MONEY SMARTS

THE GUIDE TO

SAVING MONEY

325 VALUABLE TIPS THAT WILL HELP YOU S·T·R·E·T·C·H YOUR DOLLARS

by David L. Scott

OLD SAYBROOK, CONNECTICUT

Library of Congress Cataloging-in-Publication Data
Scott, David Logan, 1942-
    The guide to saving money / by David L Scott.
        p. cm. — (Money smarts)
    Includes index.
    ISBN 1-56440-871-X
    1. Finance, Personal. 2. Saving and thrift. I. Title. II. Series:
Scott, David Logan, 1942- Money Smarts.
HG179.S3443 1996
332.024—dc20   95-52630
                                                                    CIP

Manufactured in the United States of America
First Edition/First Printing

Contents

Introduction

Money smarts begins with an appropriate state of mind. You must have an ongoing interest in saving money in order to be successful in the endeavor. You also need a little common sense and a lot of persistence, as well as the desire and willingness to seek out the good deals. Only so many good deals will fall into your hands by accident. You must be able to recognize one when you see it. Although good deals are generally available, you must make the effort to locate them.

Money smarts also requires that you *really* consider the cost of something. Each time you get ready to spend money, ask yourself if you are making a wise expenditure. Do you really need what you are about to purchase? Do you prefer this item to other things you would like to have? Every purchase entails a tradeoff. Acquiring one thing means you are deciding to give up something else. Recognizing and evaluating this tradeoff is a key element to money smarts.

Money smarts requires a certain amount of knowledge. Become informed regarding the best places to purchase goods and services. Read the local newspaper for up-to-date knowledge of the prices that are being charged in your community. Subscribe to a magazine such as *Consumer Reports* for information about the quality of various goods and services. Understand your personal finances better by reading a financial publication such as *Kiplinger's Personal Finance Magazine*. Subscriptions to both of these publications are worthwhile expenditures.

The Guide to Saving Money will give you one leg up on getting the best deals by providing some money-saving ideas you may have overlooked or not even have considered. Each idea is written in easy-to-understand language and generally includes help for putting the idea to use. You will discover ideas for saving money on transportation and housing expenditures. You may be able to use the dozens of suggestions for reducing the taxes you are required to pay. You will also find ideas that should allow you to reduce the amount of your money that is being devoured in insurance premiums. *The Guide to Saving Money* contains many ideas on how to better manage and invest your money, including a miscellaneous collection of money-saving tips, any one of which is likely to save much more than the price of this book.

I want to thank my wife, Kay, who humors me by generally allowing me to practice what I preach. I also want to thank all the employees at the Globe Pequot Press, especially my editor, Mace Lewis, who assisted in the publication of the Money Smarts series. They have always made Kay and me feel like members of the family.

David L. Scott
Valdosta, Georgia

CHAPTER 1

Credit Money Smarts

Intelligent credit management requires both understanding and discipline. Understanding credit terms and borrowing costs helps you to obtain the right loan and best terms when you borrow. Discipline is required to control spending so that excessive borrowing is avoided. The credit card you choose to use can result in major savings. Pay off high-interest credit cards as soon as possible. Consider a home equity loan to meet short-term borrowing needs.

Use a credit card that pays you. The competition among credit card companies has become so intense you can actually nab some freebies if you are choosy about the card you use. A number of issuers award airline frequent flier points based on the amount charged each month. The points can be accumulated and traded for free airline tickets. Other issuers offer cash rebates, free gasoline, credits on a new car purchase, credit toward computer purchases, and credit to a tax-deferred annuity. Rebates generally range from 1 to 5 percent of the amounts you charge. Be aware that cards offering the best rebate deals frequently entail annual fees or high interest rates. Depending on how you manage card use (for example, whether you avoid interest charges by paying the entire balance each month), the rebate on a particular card may not offset the high interest or annual fee. Some cards offering rebates are:

1. Apple Citibank MasterCard or Visa ($20/year): Credits of up to $500/year on Apple hardware and software (800–374–9999)

2. Discover Card (free): Cash rebates of 1/4 of 1 percent to 1 percent of amounts charged (800–347–2683)

3. GM MasterCard (free): Credits of up to $500/year toward purchases of GM vehicles (800–947–1000)

4. Ford Citibank Visa or MasterCard (free): Credits of up to $700/year toward purchases of Ford products (800–374–7777)

5. Shell MasterCard (first year free; then $20 annually): Credits of up to $70 annually toward Shell gasoline purchases (800–373–3427)

6. GE Rewards MasterCard (free): Discount coupons and

"reward checks" for use at selected retailers (800–437–3927)

7. Exxon MasterCard (free): Credits toward Exxon gasoline purchases (800–937–3996)

8. BP Oil Visa (free): Credits of up to $300/year toward BP gasoline purchases (800–425–7238)

9. Volkswagen Visa ($20): Credits of up to $700/year toward the purchase of Volkswagen products

Limit the number of credit cards you hold. Holding more than a few credit cards offers few benefits but has the potential to cause substantial grief. Nearly any business that accepts credit cards will accept a Visa or MasterCard issued by any financial institution. Why carry six or eight cards when you need only one? The more credit cards you own the more likely you are to misplace one, especially if several cards are seldom used. It might be months before you even realize that one is missing. You are also more likely to incur a late charge by forgetting to pay one or more of several monthly statements. Additional cards facilitate overborrowing. You're up to the limit on one card? No problem, just pull out one or more of the cards held in reserve. Take a big step in the right direction and streamline your financial life by minimizing the number of credit cards you hold.

Shop ahead for the financing required to purchase a new or used vehicle. Significant differences nearly always exist among available vehicle financing deals. Banks, credit unions, savings-and-loan associations, and vehicle dealers aggressively promote themselves in order to attract potential borrowers who are in the market to purchase a new or used vehicle on credit. It is to your benefit to nail down the most advantageous financing deal *prior to* shopping for a vehicle. This puts you in the driver's seat with respect to both the financing and the purchase. If you wait to arrange the financing until after you have struck a deal on a new car or truck, you will more likely accept the financing terms offered by the seller. After all, you will probably be in a hurry to show the new purchase to your family and friends. Arrange the needed financing while you have time to comparison shop among lenders.

Consider tapping your savings to pay off high-cost debt. The rate of interest you pay on most debts is likely to be substantially higher than the return you earn on savings. For example, many credit card companies charge annual interest rates of 15 percent and above, a level that is much higher than the typical return earned on most types of savings. Also consider that the return you are able to retain is reduced by federal and state income taxes you must pay on investment income. Savings that earns 8 percent has an aftertax return of only 6 percent if you pay taxes at a 25 percent rate. You would need an *after-tax* return of 15 percent to justify not using this savings to pay off credit card debt on which you are charged 15 percent. Suppose the outstanding balance on your credit card(s) averages $1,400. Assuming a 15 percent interest rate, you are paying annual interest of .15 times $1,400, or $210. This interest expense is not permitted as a deduction in calculating your income taxes. Now suppose your savings is earning a pretax return of 6 percent, meaning that you earn $84 in interest income on $1,400 of the savings. Even the lowest federal income tax rate of 15 percent will require that you pay taxes of

$12.60 on the investment income, leaving only $71.40. Thus, withdrawing $1,400 from your savings to pay off the credit card balance will save $210 in interest charges at the same time it reduces your aftertax interest income by $71.40. The result is that you save $138.60 annually.

Take a copy of your credit file along when you apply for a loan. Lenders often charge loan applicants a stiff fee to check their credit history. The fee may have little to do with the actual expenses the lender incurs. It is just another method of squeezing a bigger profit from a loan applicant. You can obtain a copy of your credit file for a nominal fee from the local credit bureau (listed in the telephone directory Yellow Pages under "Credit Reporting Agencies"). At the same time you complete the loan application, include a copy of your credit file and request that the lender forego the normal fee for a credit check.

Don't accept a credit card company's offer to defer or reduce your monthly payment. Credit card companies sometimes offer cardholders the opportunity to skip a month's payment or to pay less than the normal minimum without penalty. Although you avoid the penalty, you are still charged interest at the normal high rate on the outstanding balance. The payment waiver actually causes you to dig yourself deeper into debt because you now have another month's interest charges added to your outstanding balance. The offer is designed to benefit the credit card company, not you. It is to your advantage to skip the "deal" rather than to skip the payment.

If you don't ordinarily pay the full amount of your out-

standing credit card balance each month, you should pay as early as possible. Different credit card companies use different methods for calculating your monthly interest charge. In general, credit card companies *do not* charge interest on your lowest balance (this would hurt their profits). Rather, they calculate interest on the average daily balance (the sum of each day's balance divided by the number of days in the billing period). This means that if you don't pay the entire balance during the grace period, you will have to pay interest not only on the balance that remains after your payment is credited, but also on any balances in your account during the entire month. In other words, the more days you wait before paying, the higher the average will be. Some companies even pick up balances from the prior month when calculating your interest charges. If you pay less than the full amount, you may well be charged interest on your account's outstanding balances *before your payment is credited.* Be certain to determine how monthly interest is calculated when you select a credit card. This warning can be ignored if you pay your outstanding balance in full each month.

Choose a credit card without an annual fee if you always pay off the entire monthly credit balance. Many credit card companies do not charge cardholders an annual fee. These firms often make up for this freebie, however, by charging a relatively high interest rate on unpaid balances. If you regularly pay the outstanding balance in full, don't worry about the interest rate the company charges because you won't be paying any interest. Unless you consider it worth a nominal annual fee to obtain a card that offers frequent flier points or some other inducement, stick with a card from an issuer that doesn't charge an annual fee.

INCREASED COST OF USING CREDIT COMPARED WITH PAYING CASH

Cash Price	Interest Rate on Loan	Payment Frequency	Payment Amount	Number of Payments	Total of Payments	Increased Cost
$10,000	6%	annual	$10,600	1	$ 10,600	$ 600
12,000	8	monthly	376	36	13,536	1,536
12,000	8	monthly	243	60	14,580	2,580
500	12	monthly	44	12	528	28
95,000	7	monthly	632	360	227,520	132,520
95,000	10	monthly	834	360	300,240	$205,240
95,000	7	monthly	854	180	153,720	58,720
3,000	9	monthly	137	24	3,288	288

Pay off your mortgage early and painlessly by making the regular payment every four weeks rather than every month. Mortgage loans generally require monthly payments. By making the scheduled mortgage payment every four weeks instead, you can accelerate the payoff date and reduce the total amount of interest you will pay over the life of the loan. This results in one extra payment (fifty-two weeks @ four weeks per payment equals thirteen payments) each year. The entire amount of the extra payment goes to reduce the principal of the loan, which results in the loan being re-paid many years prior to the scheduled payoff date. The extra annual payment has the same effect as making payments that are larger than required. Before making the extra payments, however, be certain that you will not be penalized by the lender for paying off the loan prior to the scheduled maturity.

Avoid cash advances on your credit card. A credit card cash advance generally entails a substantial cost, usually in the form of additional interest charges. Some card companies levy a "transaction fee" rather than an interest charge. In other cases you may be required to pay both interest and a transaction fee. If interest is charged, the clock starts on the date you obtain the cash advance, not on the date the monthly payment is due. You can be assured that whether the card issuer charges a fee or interest, the cost to you will be high. If you need cash, use an ATM or debit card that immediately charges your checking or savings account for the funds you obtain. Cash advance transactions using these cards are generally free or entail only a nominal fee (typically, $1.00). Using a credit card rather than an ATM card to obtain a cash advance because you don't have a balance in your account means you need to reduce your spending.

If you typically carry a credit card balance, shop aggressively for a credit card issuer that charges a low interest rate. Annual interest rates charged by credit card issuers span a wide range from the high teens to the single digits. The rate your card company charges has a major impact on the interest charges you incur and the size of your payments, especially if you typically carry large unpaid balances. Suppose your average unpaid credit card balance is $1,500. If your card issuer charges an annual interest rate of 18 percent you will incur yearly interest charges of $270 (.18 times $1,500). The same monthly balance on a card that charges interest at an annual rate of 12 percent will result in yearly interest charges of only $180, a $90 annual saving. A larger credit balance or a lower interest rate produces even greater interest savings. Once you locate an issuer that charges a relatively low interest rate, inquire about transferring the outstanding balance from your old account to the new account. The issuer of the new card will take care of the transfer.

Ask a lender if automatic payments qualify you for a discount on interest charges. Lenders sometimes reduce the interest rate on loans when monthly payments are made with automatic deductions from a checking or savings account. An automatic-payment agreement saves you the monthly chore of writing a check and mailing a payment. It also assures the lender of timely payments on your loan. The lender generally requires that your checking or savings account be maintained at the same institution from which the loan is obtained, so you may have to move your account. The hassle of moving an account becomes more justifiable the larger the amount of the loan and the larger the reduction in the interest rate.

Check the accuracy of your credit report. It is to your advantage to periodically check the accuracy of your credit report. Individual credit files maintained by credit-reporting agencies (credit bureaus) sometimes contain incorrect information that causes substantial grief. Most commonly, information meant for the credit report of some other person with your name mistakenly ends up in your credit file. You can only locate erroneous entries if you examine your own file. You are permitted free access to your credit file in the event that negative information in the file causes you to be turned down for credit; otherwise you may have to pay a nominal fee. If you wish to dispute information contained in the report, use the process for resolution set forth in the credit report. Credit bureaus are required to verify any information you dispute, provided you notify the bureaus within a reasonable period. If a dispute is not resolved in your favor, you are permitted to write a statement of up to 100 words that will be included in your file and sent to potential lenders who ask for your credit report. The three major national credit-reporting agencies are Equifax (800–685–1111), TransUnion (313–524–2222), and TRW (800–682–7654). TRW allows one free report per year, even when you have not been turned down for credit.

Reduce the outstanding balances on your credit cards. Interest rates on credit card balances are likely to be higher than interest rates on any of your other outstanding loans. In addition, interest paid to credit card companies is not deductible when calculating federal income taxes. If you have outstanding balances on several credit cards, first pay down the balance on the card with the highest interest rate. Check your monthly statements if you aren't certain of the interest rates you are being charged. If you are unable to locate the information on your statement, use the card issuer's toll-free phone number and ask someone at the company. Large credit card balances at high interest rates can bleed your paycheck to the point that you haven't enough money left to take care of regular living expenses. The best deal is to make certain credit card balances are paid in full each month. Running up credit card balances is a lot like smoking cigarettes; once you begin it's difficult to stop. If you don't start, you won't miss it.

Shop for the lowest cost on a loan. All lenders are not created equal. Lenders don't enjoy the same cost of funds, efficiencies, or lending philosophies. Some lenders make up for low credit standards with high interest rates. Other lenders, who are more selective in the loans they make, are able to charge lower interest rates. Many consumers go to great lengths to obtain the lowest possible price on furniture, automobiles, and home repairs and then accept whatever financing is offered. You can often save as much or more by shopping for financing as you can by shopping for what you intend to purchase on credit. The more you plan to borrow and the longer a loan will remain outstanding, the more you can save by shopping for the lowest cost on a loan. Significant differences in costs are often available on automobile loans, home loans, credit card borrowing, and personal loans. Remember as well that interest may not be the only cost of borrowing money. Lenders may levy separate charges such as fees for loan applications and credit reports. Interest charges and other expenses associated with most types of loans cannot be used as deductions to reduce your tax liability. Do yourself a favor and shop for credit.

Obtain all the facts before consolidating your debts. Debt consolidation involves entering into an agreement with a lender who establishes a new loan out of which some or all of your existing debts are paid off (mortgage loans are generally excluded). Credit card balances and outstanding balances on other personal loans are paid off by the lender while you make a single monthly payment on the new loan. The new monthly payment is frequently lower than the sum of the monthly payments on the loans that have been paid off. Debt consolidation sounds like a no-brainer. In fact, it may be a good deal if the interest rate on the consolidation loan is lower than interest rates being charged on the loans it would repay. Unfortunately, the reduced monthly payment on the new loan may result from an extended schedule of payments, with an interest rate that is actually higher than interest rates being charged on the old loans. A higher interest rate combined with a greater number of payments means you pay more, rather than less, total interest on a consolidation loan. If you are thinking about debt consolidation be certain to check not only the size of your monthly payments, but also on the interest rate you will be charged and the number of payments that will be required.

Talk with your creditors if you are experiencing difficulty making loan repayments. Your creditors have an interest in your financial stability. After all, they want the money they are owed. If you are unable to make loan payments because you have been laid off your job or you have been sick and unable to work, call or visit your creditors to discuss the problem. You may find that they are not as hard-nosed as you might expect. They may be willing to let you miss a payment or two or to reduce the size of the required payments by extending the repayment period. This will give you some breathing room without monetary penalties or the report of negative information to a credit bureau. Your creditor may also be able to refer you to a credit counseling firm. Be aware, however, that the longer you wait to talk with creditors, the less willing to compromise they are likely to be.

Consider all credit charges when you shop for a loan. Federal law requires that creditors disclose the dollar cost of credit and the annual percentage rate (APR) *before* credit is extended. The disclosure allows you to compare the cost of credit for loans with different terms from the same lender and from different lenders, and to choose the loan and the lender that provide the best deal. The dollar cost of credit includes the total of all the charges you will be required to pay, including interest, loan fees, service charges, credit investigation fees, and premiums for credit life insurance. When you compare the cost of credit among different loans, make certain you are evaluating comparable loans. Loans of the same principal and the same length are easiest to compare.

Ask your credit card company for a lower rate of interest. If you are a regular credit card user who maintains an outstanding balance and regularly meets the minimum payments, you are a candidate for a lower interest rate. The interest rate charged by a credit card issuer isn't set in stone. In fact, these firms regularly charge different rates to customers residing in different states. Ask the financial institution that issued the card to reduce the interest rate charged on your outstanding balances. Your request may be refused, but you won't know unless you are willing to ask. The credit card business is very competitive, and issuers find it a lot cheaper to retain existing customers than to attract new ones.

Take out a home equity loan. Home equity loans have one terrific advantage over nearly all other types of consumer debt: the interest charges qualify as itemized deductions in calculating your federal (and probably state) income tax liability, even if the proceeds of the loan are used for purposes unrelated to your home. For example, you can deduct inter-

---

EFFECTIVE INTEREST RATE FOR DIFFERENT LOAN PAYMENT SCHEDULES

Suppose you approach several different lenders with the same request: to borrow $3,000 for one year. Each lender quotes an interest rate of 10 percent but offers different repayment plans.

Lender 1 The lender adds interest of $300 to the loan principal of $3,000 and requires you to make a single payment of $3,300 at the end of one year.

Lender 2 The lender gives you $3,000 and requires 12 equal monthly payments of $265.85. Each payment takes care of the monthly interest charge and causes a slight reduction in the amount owed.

Lender 3 Lender adds $300 interest to $3,000 borrowed and divides by 12 to obtain monthly payments of $3,300/12, or $275. You receive $3,000.

Lender 4 Lender keeps interest of $300 and gives you $2,700. Payments are set at $3,000/12, or $250.

Lender	Amount Borrowed	Payments	Total Payments	Total Interest Paid	Approximate Interest Rate
1	$3,000	$3,300	$3,300	$300	10.00%
2	3,000	263.75/month	3,165	190	10.15
3	3,000	275.00/month	3,300	300	18.46
4	2,700	250.00/month	3,000	300	20.51

est charges on a home equity loan even if you use the proceeds of the loan to purchase an automobile. In contrast, interest you pay on credit card debt, school loans, personal loans, and automobile financing is not tax deductible. Deductible interest can reduce the cost of borrowing by from 28 to 40 percent, depending on your federal income-tax bracket. Being allowed to deduct these interest charges on your state tax return is an added bonus. Several regulations should be kept in mind when you are considering a home equity loan. First, you can only deduct interest on the first $1 million of mortgages. Second, only loan interest on your main home and one other home qualifies for this tax deduction. Third, if you refinance an existing mortgage, interest on the new mortgage qualifies for the deduction only to the extent that the new mortgage does not exceed the old mortgage. Fourth, the loan must be secured by your primary home or a vacation home.

Ask your credit card company to waive its annual fee. The increasing availability of credit cards without an annual fee may make it possible for you to obtain a waiver of the annual fee on your own card just by asking. Tell the card's issuer that you have received several offers from other issuers that don't charge an annual fee. You have nothing to lose. The worst that can happen is to be told no.

If you have to take out a five-year car loan to be able to afford the loan payments, you need to purchase a less expensive vehicle. Lenders have extended the length of car loans from three years to four years and, finally, to five years in order to keep loan payments within the reach of many car buyers. A three-year loan allows you to own something of value when the loan has been repaid. At the end of a five-year loan you own a vehicle, but it is unlikely to have much value. Being unable to make the payments on a three- or four-year loan to buy the vehicle you want probably means that you need to consider vehicles more in line with your financial resources. Remember, a less expensive vehicle is likely to mean greater mileage, less depreciation, less maintenance, and lower insurance premiums. If you are already financially strapped to make loan payments, the last thing you need is a vehicle that is costly to operate.

Generally avoid retail charge accounts. Many retail establishments, especially department stores, maintain their own charge account programs. Like a regular credit card account, you are permitted to charge up to an established maximum (your credit line) and either pay the entire balance or make monthly payments. Retail charge accounts generally entail relatively high interest rates and offer no advantages over charge cards you may already hold. Nearly all retailers now accept national charge cards. If you carry a charge card that offers a benefit such as frequent flier points or credits for gasoline or a new vehicle, it is to your advantage to use this card rather than the retailer's card. Avoiding retail charge accounts also reduces the number of cards you have to carry and keep track of.

If your credit card provides frequent flier credits or a rebate, charge everything. Some card issuers provide rebates of 1 to 3 percent or frequent flier credits for the amount you charge. The more purchases you charge the more rebates or frequent flier credits you earn. Assuming you have the financial resources and discipline to pay off your balance at the end of each month, you should charge every purchase. When you purchase something, make it a point to ask if the seller accepts payment by credit card. Charge your groceries (an increasing number of grocery stores accept payment by credit card), newspaper subscription, college tuition, charitable contributions, magazine subscriptions, part or all of a vehicle purchase (if no surcharge is added), a plumbing bill, service on your vehicle, and every other purchase. When you charge everything it doesn't take long to accumulate sufficient credits for a free airline flight, a significant discount on a new vehicle or computer, or free gasoline. Disregard this advice if you lack the financial discipline required to make your payments in full and on time.

If your credit card provides a rebate but the amount of the rebate is limited, apply for an additional card. Credit cards with rebates on purchases often limit the dollar amount in rebates you can obtain during a year. For example, the Shell MasterCard® provides 2 percent rebates on annual purchases up to $3,500 ($70 in rebates). Charges exceeding this amount earn nothing. Beat this system by having your spouse apply for a separate card in his or her name. Likewise, the two of you might apply jointly for a card. Opening another account in your spouse's name will allow you to continue to enjoy benefits after you have reached the maximum on your current card. If you are single and are likely to exceed the rebate limit on your card, apply for a rebate card from a different issuer.

Reduce interest charges by juggling credit card balances from one card to another. Credit card companies often offer special low interest rates during the first three to six months after an account is opened. For example, a card company may offer an annual interest rate of 5 percent on unpaid balances during the first six months you own the card, and thereafter increase the interest rate to 14 percent on unpaid balances. Many card issuers offer this incentive to convince you to apply for their card and to move outstanding balances from your existing cards to the new account. If you typically carry a relatively large balance on your credit card (a bad idea), you may as well apply for one of these other cards and transfer your outstanding balance, usually by means of a check from the new card issuer. After transferring the outstanding balance, begin looking for yet another card that offers the same incentive (that is, a low introductory rate) so you will be able to transfer the balance just before the interest rate is increased on your second card. Repeating this process allows you to turn what is normally a high-cost source of credit into a low-cost source of credit. Keep in mind that the best policy is to avoid unpaid balances, not to shuffle balances.

Charge items likely to need repair with a credit card that provides an extended warranty feature. Some credit cards include a bonus feature that doubles the warranty (up to an additional year) on products purchased with the card. The extra warranty coverage is provided by the card company rather than by the manufacturer. Limitations may be imposed on these extra warranties. For example, they may stipulate a maximum price or limit the length of the original warranty on any given purchase. Limitations are explained in the extended warranty agreement supplied by the card company. Because these cards rarely include rebates or frequent-flier points, you should not use them to charge items such as groceries and clothes, where warranties don't exist.

Pay cash for goods, borrow to invest. The tax code is written in such a way that you benefit when you borrow money to pay for investments but not when you borrow money to buy goods and services. Interest you pay on a loan used to acquire investments is deductible on your federal income taxes, but interest you pay on a loan whose proceeds are used to purchase goods and services is not. Thus, rather than paying cash for your investments and borrowing to buy an automobile, you should pay cash for the automobile and borrow to purchase the investment. Keep in mind that deductions for interest expense on loans to finance investments are limited to the amount of investment income you earn.

Choose a credit card over a debit card. Debit cards look exactly like credit cards but provide no payment deferral. Use of a debit card results in an immediate deduction of funds from your checking account. A credit card purchase generally does not require payment for twenty-five to sixty days following the purchase. It is to your advantage to pay later, because your funds can earn interest for another twenty-five to sixty days. As a finance person would say, "Your money is working for you longer." Debit cards at one time offered the advantage of no annual fee, while credit card issuers typically charged $25 to $100 annually. However, the credit card business is now so competitive that many issuers no longer charge an annual fee. Choose a no-fee credit card and benefit from the payment deferral. Don't forget to pay your credit card bills on time.

Judge a loan by more than the size of the payments. You may have received a loan solicitation in the mail that offered you a $2,500 check in return for agreeing to make seemingly nominal monthly payments. The nominal payments probably obscured what was, in reality, an expensive loan.

The payback on a loan is a function of both payment size and the number of payments. Don't agree to borrow money merely because the payments seem reasonable. Rather, consider the overall finance charges (the amount you repay that exceeds the amount you borrow) and the annual percentage rate (APR) on the loan, both of which must be disclosed in the agreement you sign. Judging a loan only by the size of its payments is like judging the cost of a box of cereal only by the size of the box. A loan with nominal payments can be incredibly expensive if the payments last for many periods.

Choose which of your credit cards to use based on the cards' billing cycles. Credit card accounts have different billing cycles and payment dates. You can determine the billing cycle of a card by checking your statement (observe when in the month the first charges of each statement took place) or by calling the credit card company. It is to your advantage to charge items at the beginning of a billing cycle because a longer period of time will elapse between the date of purchase and the date you are required to pay the monthly bill. For example, if your billing cycle ends on the first Tuesday of each month, any charges subsequent to that date will not be due for payment until twenty-five days (usually) after the billing cycle ends. Any purchase you charge near the beginning of a billing cycle will not be due for payment for nearly two months! If you intend to make a relatively large credit transaction, wait to use the card until just after a billing cycle ends. If you have two cards with different billing cycles, choose which card to use on the basis of which will provide the later payment date. Remember, time is money!

Leave your credit card at home. If you lack the financial discipline to regulate your spending, make it a point *not* to carry your credit card(s) with you. Leave your cards at home, tucked in a safe place where they are available, but not too available. Credit cards hidden out of sight and out of your pocketbook will soften the temptation to make purchases you cannot afford. Carry a credit card only when you know you will need credit to make a specific purchase.

Don't pay extra for a premium credit card. Most credit card issuers offer a premium version of their credit card at a higher annual fee. For example, a bank may offer a regular credit card at no annual fee, but charge $25 annually for a gold card. Another issuer may levy an annual charge of $25 for a regular card and $50 for a gold card. Don't waste money on the premium card unless it offers benefits that are worth the extra cost. No one who accepts the card for payment will care about the color, so why should you? Although prestige cards usually offer a higher credit line, you can almost always obtain a higher credit line on a regular card on request. Weigh the benefits of a prestige credit card before you agree to pay the extra freight. Chances are you are better off with the cheaper version.

Record credit card charges in your checkbook register. If the bottom line of your monthly credit card statement(s) comes as a major surprise, you may find it helpful to record each credit card purchase in your checkbook register. At the same time you record a purchase, deduct the amount of the purchase from the balance in your account. As long as the balance of your account remains above zero, your checking account contains sufficient funds to allow you to pay the full amount of your monthly credit card bill. On the other hand, a negative balance in your checking account balance indicates that you will be unable to pay your monthly credit card bill without withdrawing funds from savings. Adjusting your checking account balance for credit card use helps you keep track of how much you are charging and whether you can afford it.

CHAPTER 2

Household Money Smarts

Shelter consumes a large proportion of most family budgets. Substantial savings is available from buying what you require rather than buying to impress others. The cost of energy is a major expense of operating a household, and major savings can be realized by implementing common-sense measures of conservation. Consider resale value when you are choosing a home to purchase.

Install a timer on your electric hot water heater. Regulating the flow of electricity to your water heater can result in significant energy savings. Installing an inexpensive electric timer (available at most discount and home improvement stores) in the electric line to your home's water heater allows you to determine the hours of the day during which water will be heated. For example, you might want to set the water heater to come on for an hour or so and then shut off before you get up each morning. A second setting might turn the water heater on for an hour or two (and then turn it off) before you return home from work. In both cases water is not being heated or kept hot during the hours you don't expect to use hot water. You shower in the morning before going to work and leave cold water in the water heater until the warming period begins just before you return home in the evening. If you or your spouse remain home with several young children most of each day, a timer will probably not be practical. Also, these timers don't work on gas water heaters. Still, if your lifestyle permits regular periods during which you use hot water, and if your home has an electric water heater, a timer can be a real energy saver.

Change long distance carriers only if you get something for your trouble. Long distance carriers are fighting tooth and nail for new customers. Competition has become so intense that some companies are willing to pay customers from $25 to $100 to switch! Sometimes you can receive substantial reductions on your long distance calls for three to six months. Get the ball rolling by calling a long distance company other than your own and asking if they are offering incentives to households that change carriers. If a representative calls and asks you to consider changing carriers, ask why you should do so. Changing carriers is such a smooth process you probably won't be able to tell when the switch occurs. Once the change is completed you are likely to be contacted by your old carrier with yet another offer if only you agree to switch back! It doesn't get any better than this!

Place a timer beside your telephone to reduce long distance charges. You may discover your long distance bills increasing even though the telephone company continues reducing its long distance rates. Larger bills result from making more and/or longer long distance calls. One way to whip your long distance bills into shape is to place a timer beside the telephone you generally use for long distance calls. This can be an inexpensive three-minute egg timer or a digital timer that you would normally use for cooking. Many people get carried away and simply don't realize how long they talk on the telephone, but lengthy conversations with friends who live far away can result in substantial charges. Each time you dial a long distance number, turn the egg timer or set the cooking timer. You may decide not to terminate the call at the end of three or five minutes, but at least you will keep track of the length of your conversation. If you use any one of several phones for long distance, invest in several timers. The timers will pay for themselves in short order.

Take advantage of energy conservation programs offered by your local utility. An increasing number of electric utilities and gas companies are offering products and services, sometimes for free, that save you (and the utility) money. Utilities sometimes offer to inspect your home, insulate your water heater, provide low-cost or free energy-saving light bulbs, or pay rebates on specified types of home improvements. These programs are often worthwhile and should be taken advantage of. Call the local office of the electric company and/or gas company and ask if any conservation programs are available in your locality.

Insulate your water heater. Water heaters are a major consumer of energy in your home, usually second only to central heating/cooling systems. The water heater consumes energy to heat water you use to shave, bathe, wash dishes, and launder your clothes. The unit also consumes energy when it warms water that has lost heat to the outside environment. Imagine the heat loss during a cold winter night if your water heater is located in an unheated garage utility room. You can inexpensively reduce heat loss from the hot water tank by installing a low-cost insulation blanket around the outside of the tank. The blankets are available at any home improvement store and at most discount stores. The installation process is relatively simple. Reduced energy expenses should pay for the insulating blanket within a year or less of installation.

Maintain financial records relating to owning your home. Tax considerations make it mandatory to retain indefinitely nearly all financial records relating to your home. Every expense regarding the "basis," or cost, of your home affects the recorded gain or loss when the home is eventually sold. As a homeowner you are also able to defer taxable gains when you purchase a replacement home and meet certain IRS regulations. Thus, records of all the expenses you incur that affect the cost basis on each home you own should be saved until you sell your last home and move to an apartment, rental home, or rest home. In particular, retain statements detailing the closing costs, receipts for home improvements, and proof of casualty losses to property you own.

Consider a professional inspection for a home you are thinking about buying. Your first home will probably be the single most costly investment you make—at least until you buy the next home. Without extensive knowledge of the home building business, you may overlook some very important (and expensive) problems that a professional would discover. The $250 or so that you will pay for a professional home inspection is small potatoes compared to the $100,000 and more that you will pay for a home. The inspector, who will prepare a written report for you, should be a member of the American Society of Home Inspectors. Ask to accompany the inspector for the two or more hours required to make a thorough inspection. Even one discovery that you would otherwise overlook (*e.g.*, the condition of the roof) can save substantially more than the cost of the inspection. To locate a home inspector, call the local Homebuilders Association, search the Yellow Pages of your telephone directory, or write to the American Society of Home Inspectors at 85 W. Algonquin Road, Suite 360, Arlington Heights, IL 60005.

Stop paying personal mortgage insurance premiums. If you bought your home without much of a down payment, the lender may have required that you purchase personal mortgage insurance that guaranteed payment of interest and principal on the loan. The insurance guarantees the lender, who is uncertain of your financial ability to handle the payments, that the terms of the loan will be met, either by you or the insurer. Although you must pay the insurance premiums (equal to about one-half of one percent of the amount borrowed), the lender is the beneficiary of the policy. When you have paid enough on the loan to reduce the outstanding mortgage balance to the point that your equity (the market value of the home less the outstanding balance on the loan) satisfies the safety needs of the lender, write to the lender and request that the insurance be discontinued. If the lender agrees, you will be able to drop the coverage and save the premiums.

Appeal the tax assessment on your home if you believe the valuation is too high. Assessors have been known to err when evaluating personal property for tax purposes. Perhaps they overvalued your home during the last regular assessment. If so, you are paying too much in property taxes. One method for judging the accuracy of your home's assessment is to compare it with the assessments of surrounding homes of similar age and size, information that is on public record. If you are uncertain where to locate current assessments of homes in your neighborhood, call local government authorities. You may discover that houses nearly identical to your own are assessed at lower values, thereby allowing the owners to pay lower taxes than you pay. If you believe your home is assessed too high, file a written complaint with the assessor's office. Be certain to support your claim with reasonable proof, such as the assessments of comparable homes.

Refinance your mortgage. Refinancing your mortgage at a reduced rate of interest is a painless method for saving substantial amounts of money. The savings you reap from refinancing your home mortgage will depend on the extent to which interest rates have declined since you obtained your current mortgage, combined with fees the lender will charge to make the new loan. The rule of thumb to refinance when the current interest rate is two percentage points less than the rate on your existing mortgage is just that, a rule of thumb. If no expenses are involved in a refinancing, savings can result from only a small decline in interest rates. In general, it is to your advantage to refinance if you can cover closing costs on the new loan in one to two years. This assumes that you plan to remain in your current home long enough to enjoy the savings. When you shop for a new loan, try to locate a lender that will preapprove the amount you need to borrow, as well as guarantee the quoted rate for the time required to finalize the loan.

If you refinance a home mortgage, choose a new loan with a term that is equal to the remaining length of your existing mortgage. Payments during the early years of a long mortgage go almost entirely toward paying interest charges. Few dollars remain to reduce the principal amount of the loan. In subsequent years, a small part of each payment goes toward reducing the principal of the loan. Only after ten or fifteen years of payments on a twenty-five-year mortgage do substantial reductions in the loan's principal finally occur. Suppose you are planning to refinance a mortgage on which you have been making payments for ten or fifteen years. If you refinance with a new twenty-five- or thirty-year loan, you begin making payments that once again go mostly toward covering interest charges. Save yourself tens of thousands of dollars in interest charges by choosing a term on the new loan that is approximately the same as the remaining length of the existing loan. If you have been paying

FACTORS FOR CALCULATING
PERIODIC SAVING TO MEET GOALS

Annual Return on Savings

Year	2%	3%	4%	5%	6%	7%	8%	9%
1	1.000	1.000	1.000	1.000	1.000	1.000	1.000	1.000
2	2.020	2.030	2.040	2.050	2.060	2.070	2.080	2.090
3	3.060	3.091	3.122	3.152	3.184	3.215	3.246	3.278
4	4.122	4.184	4.246	4.310	4.375	4.440	4.506	4.573
5	5.204	5.309	5.416	5.526	5.637	5.751	5.867	5.985
6	6.308	6.468	6.633	6.802	6.975	7.153	7.336	7.523
7	7.434	7.662	7.898	8.142	8.394	8.654	8.923	9.200
8	8.583	8.892	9.214	9.549	9.898	10.260	10.640	11.030
9	9.755	10.160	10.580	11.030	11.490	11.980	12.490	13.020
10	10.95 0	11.460	12.010	12.580	13.180	13.820	14.490	15.190
15	17.290	18.600	20.020	21.580	23.280	25.130	27.150	29.360
20	24.300	26.870	29.780	33.070	36.790	41.000	45.760	51.160
25	32.030	36.460	41.650	47.730	54.860	63.250	73.110	84.700
30	40.590	47.580	56.080	66.440	79.060	94.460	113.300	136.300

for ten years on a twenty-five-year loan, choose to refinance with a fifteen-year loan. Loans with a shorter term involve slightly higher payments, but the extra goes to reduce the balance of the loan. Another potential advantage is that intermediate-term mortgages often carry even lower interest rates than twenty-five-year loans.

Make ease of resale a major consideration in the purchase of a home. If you are considering the purchase of a new home be certain to consider resale value. Location and the values of surrounding homes are two important factors that should be considered. You may think that a home you find particularly attractive will also interest everyone else, but just because you like something doesn't mean everyone else will. Perhaps you are thinking of buying or building a "dream home" that you don't plan to sell. What if you lose your job? If you are close to retirement, what if you become ill or simply get tired of taking care of the yard and other maintenance? Maybe the home you select is in a beautiful but remote location. How will you feel about the home when you are in your seventies and want to be near medical care? In other words, circumstances can always change and cause you to want to sell even your "dream" home. Failing to consider ease of resale may leave you sorely disappointed in the price you can command if you decide to move.

Choose the best combination of interest rate and points on your mortgage loan. Financial institutions offering mortgage loans often offer several combinations of interest rates and points. Points are prepaid interest with each point equal to one percent of the amount borrowed. The greater the points you are willing to pay, the lower the interest rate charged on the loan. Conversely, a loan with no points is likely to have an above-average rate of interest. The key element when choosing between fewer points and a lower interest rate is the length of time you expect to live in the home or the length of time before you expect to refinance the loan. If you are relatively certain that you will be living in the same home for many years, it is generally to your advantage to choose the lower interest rate, even though you must pay more points. To determine which option to choose, calculate the length of time it will take lower loan payments to pay off the points that are charged. The shorter the payoff, the better the choice with points and a lower interest rate.

If you purchase a home for less than the sale price of your previous home, make improvements to the new home within two years of the sale of the previous home. You must purchase a home at a price that is at least equal to the sale price of your previous home in order to defer all the capital gains on the home you sell. You can increase the purchase price (for tax purposes) of your new home by undertaking improvements that add to the home's value if the improvements occur within two years of the sale of your previous home. Suppose you sell your home for $125,000 and purchase another home for $110,000. If you subsequently add a bedroom and remodel the kitchen and bathroom at a cost of $25,000, the cost of your new home will be $110,000 plus $25,000, or $135,000, and any capital gain on the sale of your previous home will be deferred.

Don't put all your financial resources in your home. A large down payment on a home purchase may be a good choice, because it will result in reduced mortgage payments and substantially lower interest expense over the life of a loan. A large down payment may also enable you to negotiate a lower interest rate with the lender. Before you make a large down payment or pay cash for a home, however, keep in mind that draining all your savings accounts and other investments places you and your family at risk in the event of an unforeseen financial problem. What if you become ill, lose your job, or face extensive repairs to your vehicle? How will you pay the bills if all your funds have been invested in your home? You should maintain a minimum level of available financial resources that can provide flexibility and security, even if doing so results in somewhat larger mortgage payments.

Keep cool with fans. It is much cheaper to operate several fans than to crank up an air conditioner, especially a central unit that cools the entire house. Fans keep you cool by increasing the airflow that helps evaporate your body's perspiration. If the increased air circulation created by a fan doesn't produce the desired effect, combine the fan with a higher-than-normal setting on your air conditioner. Rather than set the thermostat on the normal 76 degrees, try a setting of 80. At night, turn off the air conditioner and place a fan in the open window of an empty room; the fan should be directed outside and the door left open. Open the windows of the rooms you wish to cool (including your bedroom) and allow the fan to draw cool air through these rooms and exhaust air through the window. Keep in mind that using a fan in this manner will draw humidity as well as cool air into the house, so the local climate must be a factor in your decision.

Consider a variable-rate loan if you plan to live in a home for only three to five years. Variable-rate mortgage loans generally offer lower interest rates, often substantially lower, than fixed-rate mortgage loans. The risk in variable-rate loans is the potential of a major increase in interest rates that produces a corresponding increase in the payments required to service the loan. The longer you expect a loan to be outstanding, the riskier a variable-rate loan becomes. If you expect to sell the home in four or five years, however, the lower current rate on a variable-rate loan may be worth the risk. Even if short-term interest rates climb, you will be out from under the loan in a matter of several years. This assumes that you will be able to sell the home, a potentially difficult task when interest rates are high. Base your choice on the interest rate differential between variable-rate and fixed-rate loans (the greater the differential, the more you should favor the variable-rate product) and the period of time you expect to own the home.

Utilize windows and shades to reduce utility bills. Lower shades during cold winter evenings to reduce infiltration of cold air, and you will simultaneously lower the cost of heating your home. Likewise, raise shades during the day and allow the sunshine to warm the inside of your home. During summer months lower shades during periods when the sun will be shining through the windows, and raise windows in the evening when the outside temperature is lower than the indoor temperature. Using windows and shades to affect the temperature inside your home is an economical way to control utility use.

Don't conduct business with an unknown contractor until you check with the Better Business Bureau. Many contractors are not shady operators, but enough of them are that you should always check into a contractor's reputation before you sign on the dotted line. Regardless of whether you are interested in new construction, remodeling, or repairs, you need to know the past performance record of the person or firm you are considering before you allow the firm to go ahead with the job. If you don't have a local Better Business Bureau, call the local electric or gas utility. Check with the Chamber of Commerce to determine if complaints have been filed by dissatisfied customers. You may also want to ask the contractor for the names of previous customers who can provide references. Reputation should be an important consideration in choosing a contractor.

TYPICAL HOUSEHOLD EXPENDITURES

Fixed Expenditures

Rent/mortgage payment
Auto loan payment
Personal loan payment
Insurance premiums
  automobile
  disability income
  health
  life
  property
Public transportation
Education
  tuition
  books/miscellaneous
Taxes
  property tax
  intangible tax
  estimated income tax
Goals
  emergency fund
  vacation
  automobile
  college
  kitchen remodeling
  retirement

Flexible Expenditures

Food
  groceries
  meals out
Clothing
Health expenses (unreimbursed)
  dental
  doctor
  medicine
Transportation
  repairs/maintenance
  gasoline
  parking/miscellaneous
Household expenses
  maintenance
  furnishings
Utilities
  gas/oil
  electricity
  telephone
  sewer and water
Personal care
Recreation
Gifts
Charitable contributions

Install a flow restrictor in your shower. An inexpensive and painless method for reducing your water and energy bills is to install flow restrictors in shower heads. You need simply to unscrew the shower head (a wrench will be required), insert the flow restrictor in the head, and replace the shower head on the pipe. A somewhat more expensive alternative is to install a new low-flow shower head, which can range in price from less than $10 to over $50, depending on the model. A flow restrictor reduces water use without reducing the force of the spray. In practice, you can reduce water consumption in half without feeling much difference. You will save not only water, but also the energy that is consumed to heat the water. If you have a solar hot water heater, savings will be nominal. If, on the other hand, your home has an electric hot water heater and you reside in an area with high electric rates, savings will be substantial. Chances are you will be able to save the expense of the restrictor within several months. A new low-flow shower head may require a year or so of use to repay your initial outlay. In either case, it's a good return on your investment, and it isn't taxable.

Don't purchase too large a home. A big home results in big expenses, not only in purchase costs, but also in maintenance. A big home costs more to insure and to heat and cool, results in higher property taxes, and requires more extensive maintenance. It may be nice to have a couple of extra bedrooms for relatives who visit once every several years (although maybe it would be nice if you didn't). Even if you welcome houseguests, consider how much it costs to have a home with several bedrooms that sit empty most of the year. Cut your housing costs by choosing to live in a small home. If you are worried about being able to resell a small home, remember that a huge number of current renters will soon be wanting just such a first home. Likewise small homes are often desired by retirees.

Negotiate a lower cap on a variable-rate mortgage loan. A variable-rate mortgage loan typically offers a lower initial interest rate compared to the rate that would be charged on a fixed-rate loan. The rate on a variable-rate loan, however, can change during the term of the loan. A decrease is no problem, of course, since it results in lower interest charges. An increase is another matter. With a variable-rate mortgage you may find yourself paying a much higher interest rate down the road than you pay initially. Most variable-rate mortgage loan agreements contain a clause stipulating the amount the interest rate on the loan can change during a given period (typically 2 percent a year) and during the term of the loan (typically 5 percent total). If you choose a variable-rate mortgage loan make certain the loan agreement specifies an interest-rate cap. When the loan agreement is being drawn up, attempt to negotiate a lower cap. Even a reduction of one half of 1 percent offers the potential of substantial savings over the term of the loan. The lower the cap, the less risky your position as a borrower.

Switch to lower wattage bulbs in lamps and lighting fixtures. Substituting 60-watt bulbs for 100-watt bulbs in five lamps or fixtures that are each on for an average of five hours per night will save 1,000 watts of electricity per evening, or 30,000 watts (30 kilowatts) of electricity per month. At a cost of 10 cents per kilowatt hour, this results in savings of $3.00 per month, or $36.00 per year. Substituting 40-watt bulbs for 60-watt bulbs would save half this amount. Reduced wattage bulbs are hardly noticeable in many lamps, especially those used for decoration rather than reading. Substituting fluorescent bulbs for incandescent bulbs will result in even greater operating efficiency and savings, although a greater initial outlay is required. The key to maximizing savings is to use the most energy-saving bulbs in lamps that are left on for the greatest period of time.

Make long-distance telephone calls during evenings, weekends, or holidays. Off-peak long-distance telephone calls are much less expensive than long-distance calls made during business hours. The size of the discounts and the periods during which the discounts apply depend on the tariff schedule of your long-distance carrier. You can usually save from 25 to 40 percent for direct dial calls made between 5:00 P.M. and 11:00 P.M. on weekdays and Sundays, and from 25 percent to 60 percent for direct dial calls made all day Saturday and Sunday until 5:00 P.M. The larger discount usually applies as well to calls placed any day between 11:00 P.M. and 8:00 A.M. Plan long-distance calls so you are able to take advantage of the reduced rates. For example, if you live on the East Coast and need to talk with someone at a business on the West Coast, call after 5 P.M. your time in order to receive the discounted rate. If you are on the West Coast and need to call a business or friend on the East Coast, place your call before 8 A.M. your time. Call friends only during periods when you receive the maximum discount. Call your long-distance carrier to verify the time periods during which discounts apply and keep the schedule beside each of your telephones as a reminder of when to place your calls.

Consider renting, rather than buying certain household

items. Some items are better rented than owned. If an item is used only once a year or once every several years it may not make sense to buy it. If you only rarely require the use of a steam sprayer or garden implement, for example, you may be better off renting than owning. Renting means you don't have to worry about maintenance or finding space to store yet another thingamajig. Before you rent, shop among several rental firms; rental prices for the same item can vary considerably. Also, consider renting what you need from a neighbor or going together with one or two neighbors to purchase a seldom-used, but expensive item. For example, you can syndicate a riding lawn mower. If you choose this route, however, be sure to work out all the details first.

Close off unused rooms. If you currently heat and cool several seldom-used rooms in your home, you are wasting energy and money. Consider closing the air ducts and doors in rooms used mostly for storage and occasionally for guests. Closing unused rooms may reduce heating and cooling costs by up to 20 percent, depending on the proportion of your home's total square footage the closed rooms comprise. Check with the dealer of the heating and cooling system in your home to determine whether closing off rooms has the potential to harm the system.

Consider temporarily suspending telephone service when you plan to be away from home for several months. Telephone companies often offer a special monthly vacation rate when you won't be using your telephone for a period of a month or more. For example, the local phone company may offer a vacation rate that is half the regular monthly fee. If a charge is imposed to resume service, you will have to determine whether the one-time charge will exceed total monthly savings from utilizing the vacation rate. The longer the period of time you will be away from home the more likely placing your telephone service on vacation rate will produce savings. If the phone company does not levy a charge to resume service, you will save money by choosing the vacation rate for even a single month. You can avoid any monthly fees by having your telephone service disconnected, but the cost of reconnection tends to be high; a relatively long period of time away from home is required to make this choice superior to the vacation rate. Determine your most advantageous choice by calling your local telephone company and obtaining all the facts.

Choose sponges and cloth towels in place of paper towels. Paper towels are a disposable product for a throwaway society. Increased use of paper towels results in thinner forests for the nation and a thinner pocketbook for you. Most jobs suitable for paper towels are also suitable for either a sponge or a cloth towel. Dry the dishes and wipe the kitchen counter with cloth towels, clean the sink and food spills with a sponge, and dry your windows with old newspapers. Save paper towels for the really messy jobs that are likely to ruin a sponge or cloth towel. Make cloth towel use more automatic by moving paper towels under the counter or to the pantry where they are out of sight.

Run your dishwasher with the heated dry cycle off. The dishwasher in your home (the automatic version, not your spouse) consumes up to a kilowatt hour of electricity when it is operated with the heated dry cycle. The heating cycle for drying utilizes a large metal rod that glows red and consumes substantial amounts of energy when it is in use. Select the off position for the heating cycle on the dishwasher control panel. If no heating switch is available, bypass the heating cycle by turning off the dishwasher at the end of the wash cycle. Your dishes will get just as clean without the dry cycle. They will simply take longer to dry. Compensate for increased drying time by operating the dishwasher before you go to bed so that the dishes can dry overnight. The drying process can be hastened by leaving the dishwasher door open at the end of the wash cycle.

Wash your clothes in cold water. You will save on energy costs and at the same time prolong the life of your clothes by washing them in cold rather than warm or hot water. A regular-size washing machine consumes thirty-one gallons of hot water when you choose the hot-wash, warm-rinse setting. A warm-wash, cold-rinse setting results in the consumption of eleven gallons of hot water. An electric water heater requires nearly eight kilowatt hours of electricity to heat thirty-one gallons of water and three kilowatt hours of electricity to heat eleven gallons of water. At a cost of 8 cents per kilowatt hour (a modest estimate), heating the water to wash your clothes costs nearly 62 cents for the hot-water wash and 22 cents for the warm-water wash. This is the savings that can be realized by choosing the cold-wash, cold-rinse cycle. Savings will be somewhat less if water is heated with natural gas. Cold wash water has the added advantage of being more gentle on the fibers of your clothing.

CHAPTER 3

Insurance
Money Smarts

Insurance is one of several methods for handling the risk of financial loss. Insurance can be an expensive alternative because insurance companies must charge premiums that cover their overhead and claims. Insurance needs for an individual change over time. Buying too much insurance and unnecessary kinds of insurance can waste substantial sums of money.

Think carefully before agreeing to include credit life insurance as part of a loan contract. Lenders often try to convince borrowers to purchase a life insurance policy that pays the balance of the loan in the event the borrower dies. Some lenders automatically include this insurance in the contract, thereby requiring that you request that it be deleted if you don't want it. Credit life policies are quite expensive for the coverage they provide compared to term life insurance purchased through regular channels. In addition, credit life premiums typically fail to reflect a borrower's age or health, making a bad deal even worse if you are young and healthy. Turning down credit life may be an easy way to save money when you borrow.

Forgo collision insurance on an older vehicle. Collision insurance reimburses you for damage to your vehicle when you are at fault or when you are unable to collect from the other party. Collision coverage for a new vehicle is expensive, but premiums decrease as your vehicle grows older and declines in value. Unfortunately, a vehicle's market value tends to decrease more rapidly than collision insurance premiums. At some point after your vehicle is six or seven years old, its market value (which is the maximum amount you stand to recover from the insurance company) may be too small to justify the collision insurance premium you are being charged. Be careful, however, about canceling this insurance when you are without any funds to buy a new vehicle.

Don't pay for insurance you don't need. Buying more insurance than you need and continuing to carry insurance policies you no longer require waste your money just as surely as when you purchase clothes you won't wear or food you won't eat. Overall, the average insurance policyholder gets back less money than he or she pays in premiums. Insurance companies use a portion of your premium dollars to pay their salespeople, to rent their opulent buildings, to provide hundreds of thousands of dollars in annual pay to many of their top executives, and to pay claims to dishonest policyholders who burn their own homes, pay crooks to steal their cars, and inflate their claims. Certain insurance coverages are necessary, even though the economics may be bad. Unfortunately, insurance agents are often much better at selling policies and informing customers of their need for additional coverage than they are at advising customers when they no longer need a particular coverage. You should occasionally review your insurance policies to identify coverages you may be able to reduce or to drop entirely.

Make certain you have adequate disability income insurance. Disability income insurance replaces a portion of your earned income in the event that you are injured or ill and unable to work. Health insurance may pay most of your medicine, hospital, and doctors' bills, but it does not cover mortgage payments (or rent), insurance premiums, college tuition for the children, or food expenses? Although you may have sufficient savings to tide you over for several months, how would you handle the bills if a serious illness kept you from working for several years? Gauge appropriate disability income coverage by the amount of your after-tax income as it relates to the expenses you and your dependents might expect to incur. Coverage equal to your gross income or even your aftertax income is rarely re-

BEST'S INSURANCE RATING CLASSIFICATIONS

A+   Superior   Insurance companies that have achieved superior over-
                   all performance and have demonstrated the strongest
                   ability to meet their obligations.

A   Excellent   Insurance companies that have achieved excellent
                   overall performance and have demonstrated a strong
                   ability to meet their obligations.

B+   Very Good   Insurance companies that have achieved very good
                   overall performance and have demonstrated a good
                   ability to meet their obligations.

B   Good   Insurance companies that have achieved good overall
                   performance and have demonstrated a good ability to
                   meet their obligations.

C+   Fairly Good   Insurance companies that have achieved fairly good
                   overall performance and have demonstrated a fairly
                   good ability to meet their obligations.

C   Fair   Insurance companies that have achieved fair overall
                   performance and have demonstrated a fair ability to
                   meet their obligations.

quired, because certain expenses can almost certainly be reduced. Minimize the cost of this insurance by choosing a policy that does not begin making payments for three months, six months, or however long you feel you could handle expenditures with your available savings.

Inquire about discounts when you buy homeowners insurance. Insurance companies regularly provide premium discounts when you meet certain established standards. For example, you may qualify for discounts on your homeowners insurance if you install a smoke detector, fire extinguisher, dead-bolt locks, or an alarm system. You may also receive discounts if your home is relatively new or if it is without a fireplace. Each insurance company establishes its own qualifiers. The agent may not mention discounts so don't be timid about asking. Premium discounts are in place to attract business and reward customers who meet standards meant to reduce the likelihood or amount of a claim. If you don't meet the specific requirements, you may be able to qualify by spending a relatively small sum of money. For example, your insurance company may reduce your premium by 5 percent if you have a smoke detector and fire extinguisher. If smoke detectors have already been installed in your home, you need only spend a relatively small amount on a fire extinguisher to qualify for substantial savings.

Designate your teenage son or daughter as the primary driver of an older vehicle. You may have learned from experience that a teenage driver causes havoc with your automobile insurance premiums. Depending on several factors, including where you reside, it is not unusual for automobile insurance premiums to increase by 50 to 100 percent when a teenage child begins driving the family cars. Insurance companies charge high premiums because teenage drivers, especially boys, are involved in a disproportionate number of vehicle accidents. You can often reduce the impact of a teenage driver on your automobile insurance premiums by designating the teenage son or daughter as the principal driver of an older car with a nominal market value. You can save even more if you feel comfortable excluding collision coverage. If you own only one or two vehicles you may be able to designate your son or daughter as an occasional driver. Discuss the various options with your insurance agent, who should be familiar with the problem.

Ask your insurance agent about discounts on your automobile insurance. Casualty insurance companies regularly offer premium discounts on automobile insurance, for example, if you have a teenage driver who has completed a driver's education course or made the school honor roll. A son or daughter away at school without a vehicle may also qualify you for a discount—a child who isn't driving your cars can't cause damage to them. Insurance companies also sometimes offer discounts on comprehensive coverage when you install an antitheft system. You may qualify for a premium discount if you purchase a vehicle with anti-lock brakes, air bags, or automatic safety belts. You are likely to qualify for a discount if you are a safe driver, drive less than a specified number of miles each year, or are insuring multiple vehicles. While many agents freely inform customers of the discounts offered by their firms, some do not; you should guard your own interests by inquiring about discounts.

Don't automatically assume you need life insurance. Some people purchase life insurance simply because everyone they know seems to have some. Maybe you need it, but then again, maybe you don't. Paying for life insurance coverage you don't need is like paying for cable service without owning a television. Life insurance is primarily designed to provide financial security for dependents, such as young children, a nonworking or handicapped spouse, or elderly parents. The need for life insurance also depends on the amount of your outstanding debts. Determine how others would get along financially if you died tomorrow and your income stopped abruptly. While many people might mourn your passing, the loss of your income and financial expertise might not be such a tragedy. This is especially true if you are single with no dependents. It may also be true if you and your spouse both work and earn approximately equal incomes; or if your spouse provides most of the family's financial support. Perhaps you have substantial life insurance coverage through your employer. Keep in mind that life insurance at your place of employment will probably be terminated if you are laid off, change jobs, or retire. When considering your choices, beware of biased advice from life insurance agents whose job it is to sell insurance.

Use large deductibles to reduce insurance premiums. The deductible in insurance coverage represents the amount of any loss you agree to absorb. A $500 deductible on your vehicle's collision coverage means the insurance company is required to reimburse you for covered damages above $500. The first $500 of the loss is your responsibility. Substantial premium savings are possible when policies include relatively large deductibles. You can save on automobile insurance by increasing your deductibles for collision and/or comprehensive coverage from $250 to $500 or from $500 to $1,000. You can reduce the premium on health insurance coverage by including a $1,000 or even a $2,500 deductible. Likewise, disability income coverage is incrementally less expensive the longer you agree to wait before the insurance company begins to reimburse you. Keep in mind, however, that a larger deductible results in greater risk, because you are agreeing to assume a greater amount of any loss. Accepting large insurance deductibles when you have relatively meager financial resources involves too large a risk. If, on the other hand, you have substantial wealth that is readily accessible, you stand to gain by purchasing insurance with large deductibles.

Stick with highly rated insurers. When you purchase insurance make certain that the insurance company will be around when it is time to file a claim. Insurance companies are regulated by the states, not the federal government, and no federal agency guarantees that an insurer will fulfill its obligations. Until recent years there was little concern about the financial stability of insurance companies. Insurers were considered to be as stable as banks and savings and loans (and look what happened to them). Financial stability is especially important when your life insurance involves a financial commitment over several decades. A guarantee that you will earn an extra quarter of 1 percent each year on the cash value of your investment isn't as important as being certain your cash value is secure. The financial rating for an insurance company can be obtained by writing to any of three major rating agencies, which assess the financial strength of life insurance companies. These are: A.M. Best Company (Ambest Road, Oldwick, NJ 08858), Moody's Investor's Service (99 Church Street, New York, NY 10007), and Standard & Poor's Corporation (25 Broadway, New York, NY 10004). Insurance company ratings by the rating agencies are also in publications carried by major public and university libraries, and available by subscription from *The Insurance Forum* (P.O. Box 245, Ellettsville, IN 47429).

If you plan to travel outside the country, be certain to determine if your health insurance policy will provide coverage. Some health insurance policies provide coverage regardless of where you are when you need medical care. Other policies specifically exclude coverage of health expenses incurred outside the country. Before departing for another country, check with your insurance agent to determine if the coverage is valid in countries you will be visiting. If it is, find out whether any restrictions or special provisions apply. For example, what receipts are required for reimbursement? Do they need to be denominated in dollars? Are you or your physician required to contact the insurance company prior to a hospital admission or prior to surgery? If coverage doesn't apply outside the United States, you will probably want to purchase a supplemental health policy for the duration of your trip. If you have an individual health insurance policy (rather than a group policy provided by your employer) and frequently travel outside the country, look for a policy that provides the coverage you require.

Choose a noncancellable and guaranteed renewable health insurance policy. Suppose, after a bout with cancer, you discover that your health insurance company is unwilling to renew your policy. Where are you going to find replacement coverage? You can expect to experience great difficulty locating an insurance company that will want your business after having experienced a serious illness, especially cancer. You can avoid such a situation by purchasing a health insurance policy that is noncancellable and guaranteed renewable to at least 65 years of age, when you will probably be covered by Medicare. This suggestion applies only if you purchase your own health insurance. If you rely on a policy provided by your employer, you are at the mercy of that policy's limitations, unless you choose to purchase a supplemental policy.

Drive your least valuable vehicle to work. Should you subject your new Corvette, Toyota Supra, Nissan 300ZX, or Mazda RX7 to the daily grind of your work schedule, or should you choose to drive your five-year old Chevrolet Lumina and leave your new vehicle in the garage? If you garage the new car during your workday and use it exclusively for pleasure, you will save wear and tear and avoid worry about the inevitable workplace dings, dents, and scratches. You will also avoid the higher premiums charged by most insurance companies on vehicles driven to work. Of course, you will have to pay higher premiums on the other, less-valuable automobile, but the premium increase should be significantly less than the increase you would pay for driving the new car to work. If the second car has only a nominal value, you might consider dropping collision and comprehensive coverage to save even more.

Generally avoid specialized health insurance policies. Special-purpose health insurance policies assist with expenses that result from specific illnesses. One popular specialized policy covers only expenses incurred for treatment of cancer. Unfortunately, a cancer policy doesn't provide financial assistance if you suffer a heart problem. You may be better off allocating health insurance dollars toward improving a comprehensive health policy rather than buying several different policies that cover specific illnesses. If you feel you need additional health insurance, increase the maximum benefits or decrease the deductible on your existing comprehensive health policy.

Regularly review your insurance coverage. Numerous factors can alter the amounts and types of insurance coverages you require. For example, general inflation increases the amount of coverage you need for virtually all types of insurance. An increase in the cost of living means that you need additional coverage for your home, your medical bills, your liability, your vehicles, and your life. In general, when living costs double, you should double most insurance coverages. Likewise, if you remodel or make an addition to your home, you will need more homeowner's coverage, and if you have another child, you almost surely will need additional life insurance. On the other hand, as your children reach maturity you will probably need less life insurance. All insurance coverage should be periodically reviewed.

Consolidate property and casualty insurance coverage. Consolidating property and casualty insurance with a single company and, if applicable, a single agent, usually reduces both your premiums and your headaches. Insurers often provide premium discounts when you insure multiple cars, for example. You are less likely to pay for overlapping coverage when you insure through a single company. Placing your auto policies and homeowners insurance with the same insurance company may allow you to obtain an umbrella liability policy. Placing all your insurance through a single agent or company may also give you more clout should one of your claims be subject to dispute. An agent is more likely to give you the benefit of the doubt on a claim when you are a good customer with several policies. Purchasing all your policies from the same firm can also result in less paperwork and fewer premium payments.

Don't assume that a life insurance company with the best deal on one type of coverage offers the best deal on all types of coverage. A life insurance company may offer the lowest premium for $100,000 of term insurance coverage for a thirty-year-old male, but be less competitive on coverage for a fifty-year-old male or a twenty-five-year-old female. Likewise, an insurance company that is very competitive on term life insurance may be less impressive on policies that build cash values. You will obtain the best deal on life insurance only by shopping among insurers for each type policy. Request premium quotations for each type coverage from each firm you contact. When considering the purchase of term insurance to supplement cash value coverage you already own, obtain quotes from other life insurance companies as well as from your current insurer.

Determine if a child away at college qualifies for insurance purposes as an occasional operator of your family vehicles. You can reap substantial savings on automobile insurance premiums by classifying a child as an occasional driver. Of course, the child must indeed be an occasional driver (most likely to occur when a son or daughter moves away to college—without one of the family cars). Requirements vary by company; most insurers offer a reduced premium only if the

Insurance Money Smarts

SUMMARY OF TYPES OF AUTOMOBILE INSURANCE COVERAGE

Type of Coverage	Persons or Property Covered	Recommended Limits
1. Bodily Injury Liability	Drivers of an owned or nonowned car who are relatives living in the insured's household.	$100,000/$300,000 or legal minimum, whichever is larger.
2. Property Damage Liability	Drivers of an owned or nonowned car who are relatives living in the insured's household. Also, cars and property damaged by an insured driver.	$100,000 or legal minimum, whichever is larger.
3. Uninsured or Underinsured Motorist	Insured family members driving nonowned cars with permission and anyone driving an insured car with permission.	$50,000/$100,000/$50,000 or legal minimum, whichever is larger.
4. Medical Payments and Personal Injury Protection	Passengers in an owned or nonowned car driven by an insured family member.	None, if health insurance is adequate.
5. Collision	Damages done to an insured car driven by anyone with permission.	$500 deductible. None on older cars.
6. Comprehensive	Insured car and its contents.	$500 deductible. None on older cars.
7. Miscellaneous	Varies.	None.

student resides at least 100 miles from home. The amount saved will depend on whether the student is male or female and on the type coverage you purchase. The more complete your coverage and the higher the premiums paid, the greater the potential savings.

Try to obtain insurance coverage through a group. Group insurance, whether life, health, or liability, is often substantially cheaper than individual coverage. You may qualify for certain types of group insurance coverage through membership in a professional organization. Insurance companies frequently establish relationships with organizations to offer the organization's members disability insurance and term life insurance. For example, members of the American Association of Retired Persons have access to group health coverage. Your employer may sponsor certain types of group insurance coverage at group rates. Don't enroll in group plans, however, without first comparing the cost with similar coverage available on individual policies. If you are relatively young and the group insurance doesn't discriminate according to age, you may find that individual coverage is actually less expensive. More than likely, however, you'll find that group coverage costs far less than comparable coverage you are able to purchase on your own.

Avoid insurance policies with narrowly defined coverages. Insurance companies can afford to offer relatively low premiums when coverage is restricted. For example, most airports house machines offering low-cost life insurance coverage for airline flight. The premium is low, but the cost is high in relation to the restricted coverage you obtain, and the payout is pitifully low. Ask yourself why you should require additional life insurance coverage just because you are taking a particular flight. If additional life insurance coverage is needed, it is needed all the time, not just for a three-hour flight. Avoid as well disability income coverage for narrowly defined injuries, health insurance policies that cover only certain illnesses, and homeowner's policies that provide coverage for limited types of losses.

If a claim on your health insurance is denied, ask why. Misunderstandings and erroneous paperwork sometimes cause health insurance companies to deny valid claims. For example, your insurer may deny a claim it identifies as "not covered" by your policy. Call or write to the insurer and inquire why the claim was not accepted. You may discover that the physician failed to accurately or completely describe the reason for the treatment. After checking with the health insurer to determine under what conditions the claim would be honored, phone your physician or hospital and explain the problem. You may decide it is worthwhile to refile the claim. Don't accept the denial of a health claim without an investigation of your own.

Don't accept an unfair settlement from your insurance company. You are not required to accept the amount your insurance company pays on a claim. The fair value of a claim is often a subjective judgment and open to dispute. There may be more than one valid opinion on the amounts you should recover for storm damage to the roof of your home, the fender of your wrecked automobile, or the theft of property from your home. An insurance company required to pay a claim will sooner err on the downside than the upside. After all, it is in the interest of the insurance company to minimize the claims it pays. On the other hand, the insurer probably doesn't want to lose you as a customer, unless you have a history of many claims. Discuss a disputed claim with your agent. The agent doesn't want to lose your business, especially if that agent handles most of your insurance. If you fail to receive satisfaction from your agent, complain to your state insurance commissioner, who will attempt to mediate the dispute. You may live in one of the states that offer binding arbitration or formal mediation to resolve disputes between insurance companies and disgruntled customers. As a last resort you can initiate a lawsuit.

Beware of switching life insurance policies. Life insurance agents sometimes try to convince policyholders to cancel existing policies (or borrow on the cash values) and buy new policies. They may claim that the new policy has a lower premium, greater coverage, or bells and whistles not in your current policy. Proceed with caution. Policy switches are often promoted by agents or their sales managers because of the commissions the new policies will earn for the agents. In the first few years in the life of a policy, a large proportion of premiums goes to pay sales commissions to insurance agents. It is to an agent's financial advantage that you acquire a new policy, even though you don't need either a different policy or additional insurance. An unethical agent may recommend that you switch policies even though that agent sold the existing policy to you. Agents for other firms have everything to gain and nothing to lose by convincing you to switch from your existing policy to a new policy from their firm. Not all insurance switches are a bad deal, but you need to be aware that a switch may benefit the agent more than it benefits you.

Don't file small insurance claims. Even though you pay insurance premiums to transfer financial risk to your insurance company, you are sometimes better off *not* filing certain claims. Large and/or frequent claims may cause the insurance company to hike your premiums or, even worse, cancel your policy. Before you file a particular claim, compare the likely amount of the recovery with the possibility of increased premiums. Different insurance companies employ different guidelines regarding rate increases and cancellations. In general, it is to your advantage not to file small claims. Ask your insurance agent about the likely effect on your premium of filing a relatively modest claim. Keep in mind that you may put yourself at risk by not filing a claim when someone is injured.

Pass on credit card insurance. Insurance to cover unauthorized charges on credit cards continues to be sold even though potential losses were restricted years ago by passage of the Consumer Credit Protection Act. Under current law the liability for charges on a lost or stolen credit card is limited to $50 or the amount charged on a card prior to notification, whichever is smaller. Thus, your potential liability is relatively small. It doesn't pay to purchase insurance. Neither is it worth the cost to have these insurance firms guarantee to notify your credit card companies of the theft or loss of your cards. You can accomplish the same task with a few phone calls, assuming you have recorded the card numbers and telephone numbers.

Generally avoid cash value life insurance as an investment. Life insurance that accumulates cash value is frequently presented by insurance agents as an investment alternative to stocks, bonds, mutual funds, and so forth. Life insurance does offer certain investment advantages, but you are probably better off keeping your insurance needs separate from your investment needs. If your intention is to build an investment portfolio, why pay for insurance coverage you may not require? Life insurance generally entails high front-end expenses that greatly devalue your investment in the event that you need a portion or all of your funds after paying premiums for only a few years. Keeping investments separate from insurance allows you to purchase the larger amounts of insurance you may require in the form of low-cost term insurance.

Pay insurance premiums annually. Insurance companies often give you the option of paying premiums annually, semiannually, quarterly, and, sometimes, monthly. In reality, paying more than once per year is like paying in installments—it costs extra. For example, an insurer may bill you $900 annually or $475 semiannually for your homeowners policy. In this instance, paying annually rather than semiannually reduces your total premium by $50. Your semiannual auto insurance premium for $475 may offer the option of making two $255 quarterly payments. The quarterly option will only work to your advantage if the added cost is small enough, say a couple of dollars. If you must borrow the money to pay annual or semiannual premiums, the correct choice is less obvious. You will need to compare the cost of your loan with the extra cost of more frequent premium payments.

Don't purchase overlapping health insurance coverage. It is a waste of premium dollars to purchase several health insurance policies that provide overlapping coverage. Should you require treatment for an accident or illness, the insurers will coordinate the benefits they pay; you are unlikely to recover more than the total of your outlays for medical care. You end up paying premiums for one or more health policies that will not be required to provide the reimbursement you expect. It is normally better to have one comprehensive health policy with high limits and comprehensive coverage than to carry several different policies that provide lesser amounts of virtually identical coverage. If you own several health policies and are in doubt as to what action to take, talk to a representative of your primary insurer about the value of other policies you carry.

If you need life insurance, investigate the low-load or no-load variety. One of the major financial disadvantages of most cash-value life insurance policies is the high sales and/or surrender charge you must pay. Most or both of these expenses can be avoided by purchasing the low-load or no-load policies sold directly by life insurance companies. Direct sale allows these firms to by-pass the commissions that must normally be paid to salespeople. You will find low-load and no-load policies advertised in consumer and financial publications that cater to cost-conscious individuals such as yourself.

CHAPTER 4

Investing
Money Smarts

An investment should be analyzed on the impact it will have on your total investment portfolio. It is important to understand the risks of an investment before committing your money. Diversification is one of the best methods for minimizing the possibility of large losses. It is wise to build a portfolio of investments that is best suited to meet your own financial goals.

Stay clear of junk bonds. Junk bonds (bonds on which payment of interest and principal are somewhat uncertain) often provide much higher returns than are available on fixed-income investments (an investment that pays a constant amount of interest or dividend income). The high yields compensate investors in junk bonds for the possibility that they will not get what they have been promised. That is, interest payments may be delayed or curtailed, and the principal may remain unpaid on the maturity date. Thus, owners of junk bonds may earn much less than they expected at the time the bonds were purchased. High-risk investments are for professional investors who are able to evaluate the risks and withstand potential losses. Most individual investors should avoid bonds that are less than investment-grade.

Participate in a dividend reinvestment plan (DRIP). Many corporations sponsor plans that permit their shareholders to choose to have their dividends automatically invested in additional shares of stock. Many of these firms pay the cost of administering the plan and absorb commissions charged to purchase shares of stock. Dividend reinvestment plans allow you to increase the number of shares you own, often at no expense to you other than the purchase cost of the shares. Most reinvestment plans also permit you to contribute additional money in order to purchase even more shares of stock. They are a convenient and inexpensive way to accumulate shares and build your stock portfolio. Several organizations offer, for a nominal fee, to arrange for the purchase of a single share of a company's stock. Owning one share allows participation in the firm's DRIP. Keep in mind that reinvested dividends remain fully taxable and will be reported to the IRS.

Save brokerage commissions by purchasing shares of common stock directly from the issuing company. Some corporations, including very large firms such as Exxon, Mobil, and Texaco, sell shares directly to investors. Buying shares directly allows you to avoid the commissions that would normally be charged by a broker. The bad news is that only a relatively small number of firms currently offer this service, so you can't build a diversified portfolio in this manner. Firms that offer this service generally require a minimum initial purchase of $250. Don't invest your savings in the stock of a company just because you are able to save a brokerage commission. Still, if you are interested in purchasing the stock of a particular company you should determine if you can buy direct and save commissions. Several firms that offer direct purchases, along with their respective telephone numbers are:

Barnett Banks (800) 446–2617
COMSAT (800) 524–4458
Dial (800) 453–2235
Exxon (800) 252–1800
Kerr-McGee (800) 786–2556
Mobil (800) 648–9291
Texaco (800) 283–9785
U S West (800) 446–2617

Consider a discount broker for buying and selling securities. Discount brokerage firms generally offer commission savings of 50 percent and more on stock transactions compared to the commissions charged by full-service brokerage firms such as Merrill Lynch, Prudential, Dean Witter, and Smith Barney. Some discount firms offer even greater commission savings. Commission savings are small on relatively small transactions (*e.g.*, 50 shares of a $20 stock). Fidelity, Quick & Reilly, and Charles Schwab are three large discount brokerage firms with offices in many large cities. Waterhouse Securities and Brown and Company are smaller but generally offer even larger savings than the three majors. All these firms have been in business for many years and each has a toll-free telephone number that can be obtained from 800 information (800–555–1212).

Don't invest in tax-exempt bonds unless you earn substantial taxable income. Most bonds issued by states, cities, counties, and political subdivisions pay interest that is exempt from federal taxation and, often, state taxation as well. These investments offering tax-free income sound inviting, but they prove to be sensible investments only if you have a large taxable income on which you pay high tax rates. Tax-exempt bonds can prove to be a bad investment choice for some investors, because they provide relatively low pretax yields compared to taxable bonds. At the same time, a high-grade taxable bond may be priced to yield $8\frac{1}{2}$ percent, a tax-exempt bond of similar risk and maturity might yield only $6\frac{1}{2}$ percent. Tax-exempt bonds have relatively low before-tax yields because they are in such great demand by wealthy investors. You should generally pay a marginal tax rate (the tax rate on an extra dollar of income) of at least 28 percent before considering investments in tax-exempt securities.

Invest in the shares of a mutual fund only after you have investigated the fees you will be required to pay. Mutual funds levy various fees that must be paid by their shareholders. All mutual funds charge their shareholders for operating ex-

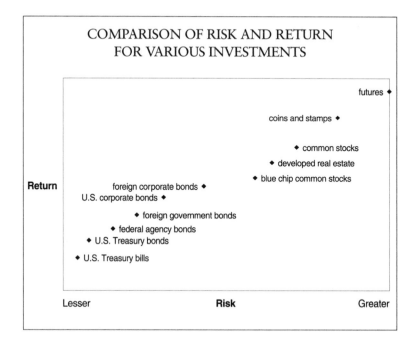

COMPARISON OF RISK AND RETURN
FOR VARIOUS INVESTMENTS

penses, an annual fee that can range from less than one half of 1 percent to more than 1 percent of a fund's assets. Low operating expenses increase a fund's yield and are an advantage for shareholders. Some mutual funds also levy either a sales fee that is added to the price of the shares you buy or a redemption fee that is taken out when shares are sold. Many mutual funds also charge a 12b-1 distribution fee. Each of these fees has the effect of reducing the return you will earn from investing in shares of a mutual fund. Although all mutual funds charge an operating fee, many funds do not levy sales or redemption charges or 12b-1 fees.

Mutual funds are required by law to provide a description of all the fees they charge. Request a *prospectus* that outlines the fees. Several business periodicals, including *Money*, *Business Week*, and *Forbes,* publish special issues that detail the fees charged by mutual funds. Keep in mind that high fees do not necessarily mean better investment performance.

Don't place all your investment eggs in one basket. Diversification is a cardinal rule of investing. Never put all, or even a large proportion, of your savings in a single asset such as real estate, stocks, bonds, a business, investment-grade stamps, or even baseball cards. No matter how much you know about something, you may make a mistake. Someone who appears to be an investment genius one year may turn into the world's greatest fool the following year. Play it safe by spreading your investment funds among dissimilar assets. Own some stocks, some bonds, some insurance, some real estate, and so forth. Of course, your ability to diversify is partly a function of the amount of investment funds available to you. The greater your wealth, the easier it is to diversify. Don't bet everything you have accumulated on the performance of a single investment asset.

Don't invest your money with someone you don't know. Unseen promoters at the other end of long-distance calls continually attempt to convince people to part with their savings by purchasing art, commodities, and low-price common stocks that offer the potential of "unbelievable" gains in value. Rooms filled with banks of telephones manned by fast-talking individuals who are equally at home selling used cars, cheap jewelry, and swamp land serve as home base to promoters who operate boiler-room operations that promote questionable investments to the greedy and the gullible. Investments promoted by telephone are often sold at huge markups that make it virtually impossible for you to earn a profit. Many of these investments have no resale market, so you may be stuck with what you purchase. Never invest your money with someone you don't know, especially if you are unable to evaluate what you are being asked to buy.

Use dollar cost averaging to invest in stocks or mutual funds. "Buy low and sell high" is the battle cry of investors everywhere. Every investor wants to buy stocks when prices are lowest. Unfortunately, few are successful. Even experienced investors find it extremely difficult—some would say impossible—to determine the best time to acquire a stock. It is all too easy to become pessimistic and drop out of the market when stock prices have experienced a lengthy decline. Historically, this has proven to be the wrong course of action. Most investors would benefit from investing equal amounts of money at regular intervals, an investment strategy termed *dollar cost averaging*. Regardless of market increases and decreases, you plow ahead and invest the same amount of money every month or every quarter, which means you buy more shares when prices are low and fewer shares when prices are high. Over an extended period you almost always do better than when you try to "play" the market.

Consider your entire portfolio when you select investments for your IRA or Keogh plan. If you regularly contribute to an IRA or Keogh retirement plan, your accumulated funds in the plan probably account for a significant portion of your investment portfolio. The assets you select for an IRA should be chosen on the basis of the types and amounts of assets you hold outside the retirement plan. Suppose you feel your total investment assets should be allocated 50 percent to common stocks, 30 percent to fixed-income investments, and 20 percent to tangible investments (most likely, real estate). An IRA comprising mostly fixed-income assets such as bonds or certificates of deposit should be considered in calculating the 50 percent, 30 percent, 20 percent asset allocation you have chosen. If you choose only fixed-income investments for your IRA, you should reduce your investment in these assets outside the IRA. Similar adjustments apply to common stocks and tangible assets if your IRA primarily includes these assets.

Establish an IRA if you qualify for making fully deductible contributions. An IRA is an excellent retirement tool, especially if you qualify to make fully deductible contributions. Current law allows you to set aside up to $2,000 annually ($2,250 if you have a nonworking spouse) and to deduct this contribution from the taxable income you report to the Internal Revenue Service *if* you meet certain standards. Currently, you may make deductible contributions if neither you nor your spouse is covered by an employer's qualified plan, or if your adjusted gross income (your income before subtracting itemized deductions and exemptions) is less than $25,000 for an individual return or $40,000 for a joint return. In addition to the reduction in current taxes that results from your contributions, taxes on the earnings from your account are deferred until withdrawals are made. Be aware that you may have to pay a 10 percent penalty on withdrawals prior to age 59½.

Consider going through a discount brokerage firm to purchase no-load and low-load mutual funds. Some discount brokers will buy and sell shares of certain no-load mutual funds without charging a transaction fee. This method for acquiring shares of these funds has several advantages: the brokerage company takes care of the transactions and maintains records of your investment activity; you can invest in several funds and have all your activity on a single statement; and you can borrow in order to leverage (magnify the effect of) your investment position. The main disadvantage is that only about 200 different funds can currently be purchased in this manner. The fund or funds you want may not be available at no commission from a discount brokerage firm because many no-load funds are not willing to pay the discount brokerage firms a fee (usually one quarter of 1 percent of the amount invested) to be included. Not all discount brokerage companies participate. Those that do include Charles Schwab (800–266–5623), Fidelity (800–544–9697), and Muriel Siebert (800–872–0711).

Consider arbitration if you think your broker ripped you off. To keep disputes out of the courts, brokerage company contracts with clients typically specify that disputes will be settled by arbitration panels rather than through the court system. Disputes involving relatively small amounts of money are typically handled by a single arbitrator, while more serious disputes are heard by a three-member panel comprised of one representative from the financial community and two outside representatives. You may represent yourself or hire an attorney. The more money in question and the more complicated the dispute, the more likely you are to require the services of someone who understands the system. Disputes may involve *churning* (over-trading in your account to generate brokerage commissions) or investing in securities that are inappropriate for your circumstances. For example, your retirement nestegg may have been depleted by option trades initiated by your broker. Arbitration is not a sure thing, however, and some feel the process is stacked against the individual investor. In fact, arbitration involves some expenses on your part, including the cost of filing and, potentially, additional expenses for the services of an attorney. In addition, your investment losses may not be your broker's fault. Depending on where a particular security was traded (*i.e.*, on an organized exchange or in the over-the-counter market), arbitration can be initiated by contacting one of the following organizations:

American Stock Exchange, 86 Trinity Place, New York, NY 10006

New York Stock Exchange, 20 Broad Street, New York, NY 10005

National Association of Securities Dealers, 33 Whitehall Street, New York, NY 10004

Beware of investing too much money in the stock of your employer. Many corporations offer to sell shares of their own stock to employees, sometimes at a bargain price. It is tempting to invest most or even all your savings in a company you know and care a lot about. After all, if company management was smart enough to hire you, the firm's outlook must be bright. Companies often offer shares of their own stock as an option in 401(k) retirement plans, believing that employees who become shareholders will feel a financial stake in the future of the firm, and so work harder with greater loyalty. While buying stock in the company that employs you has some points in its favor, it also has a great risk. Investing in your employer puts both your savings and your job on the same chopping block. If your company experiences financial difficulties and your job becomes less secure, the value of the firm's stock is likely to decline at the same time. If things really turn bad for the company, you may lose your job and also experience a major loss on your investment. To reduce financial risk invest most of your savings in the stock of companies outside the industry in which you work. A diversified mutual fund is a good choice if this option is offered by your employer as part of its 401(k) plan.

Don't purchase a mutual fund just prior to a capital distribution. Mutual funds are not required to pay income taxes on the interest and dividends they receive, or on the capital gains they realize when investments owned by the funds are sold at a gain. Federal regulations require that mutual funds distribute gains to their shareholders who, in turn, must report the distributions as income and pay the appropriate income taxes. Capital distributions are generally made once annually, usually near the end of each calendar year. If you purchase shares of a mutual fund just prior to a capital distribution, you will be required to report the distribution as income and pay the appropriate federal taxes (and perhaps state taxes also) at a rate of 15 or 28 percent. The tax rate on short-term capital gains distributions can result in a tax rate of up to 39.6 percent. One widely held mutual fund in June and December of 1993 distributed nearly 15 percent of its net assets to shareholders, who were then required to pay taxes. Had you purchased shares in this fund just prior to the June distribution and held the shares through the end of the year you would have had to pay taxes the following

April on 15 percent of your investment. Purchase shares after, rather than before, a distribution. Telephone a fund prior to making an investment and inquire about any forthcoming distribution.

Beware of investing in the shares of a mutual fund that restricts its investments to a single industry. With nearly 7,000 different mutual funds seeking investors' money, fund sponsors are continually searching for new features to differentiate themselves from the masses. An increasingly popular method is for a fund to specialize in investments of a particular industry, such as utilities, oil companies, computer software firms, or pharmaceutical companies. These funds, sometimes called *sector funds*, offer the potential for large returns, but they also create greater risk, because all their eggs are in the same investment basket. The stock prices of companies in the same industry tend to move together. A major pitfall of investing in sector funds is that individual funds tend to become very popular after equity investments in their respective industries soar in price. The hotter a sector fund's performance, the more investors who jump on the bandwagon. This is likely to be just prior to a major correction or price decline. The bottom line is that you should steer clear of sector funds unless you are an experienced investor who understands and is willing to accept high risk.

Generally avoid investments in preferred stock. Like common stock, preferred stock represents ownership in a corporation. This type of stock gains its name from the preferential dividend distributions its stockholders enjoy compared to common stockholders of the same company.

Owners of preferred stock also have preference over common stockholders in the event the firm is liquidated. On the negative side, dividends to preferred stock investors are generally fixed in amount (i.e., so many dollars and cents per share) so that preferred stockholders are unable to participate in a firm's success. Also, preferred stockholders are limited in the amount they are to receive in the event the firm is liquidated. Although preferred stock is technically a type of equity, its market value behaves more like a long-term bond that has fixed interest payments. Further, dividend payments to preferred stockholders is subordinate to all of a firm's interest obligations. The fixed current income and greater risk would be acceptable if preferred stocks provided a high enough yield. However, because of special tax considerations available to corporate owners, the prices of preferred stocks are bid up to the point where yields are often no better than the yields that can be earned on bonds with equal credit quality. When investing for current income you are likely to be better off buying bonds than shares of preferred stocks. Beware that a broker doesn't try to steer you to a high-yielding preferred stock that is substantially more risky that you realize.

Don't put money into an investment you don't completely understand. If you don't have a fundamental understanding of a particular investment, the investment is probably too complex and risky for you to own. Newspapers often report of investors who have lost substantial sums of money in complicated and exotic investments they didn't understand. Fast-talking and unethical brokers make these investments sound too good to pass up. Options, futures contracts, penny stocks, partnerships, and new common stock issues

STOCK MARKET INDICATORS

Numerous stock market indicators attempt to measure the performance of the entire stock market. Stock market indicators are of interest to investors who want to determine how the stock market is performing. Other investors use stock market indicators as a standard against which to measure the performance of their own stock portfolios. The indicators vary in the size of the samples used, in the types of stocks included, in the weighting given to each stock, and in the method of calculation. Some of the most popular stock market indicators are described below.

Dow Jones Industrial Average (DJIA or the Dow)—The oldest and most frequently quoted indicator is comprised of 30 stocks of some of America's largest and best-known industrial corporations. The Dow is calculated by adding the market prices of the 30 stocks and dividing the sum by a number that takes account of changes in the makeup of the indicator. Dow-Jones publishes separate specialized indicators for utility and transportation stocks.

Standard & Poor's 500 Index (S&P 500)—A popular indicator with financial analysts who consider it to be a more accurate gauge of stock market movements than is the DJIA. The S&P 500 uses the market value (stock price times number of shares outstanding) of 500 stocks and is calculated using a 1941–43 base of 10. Standard & Poor's publishes other specialized indexes.

New York Stock Exchange (NYSE) Index Series—A series of five indexes that are calculated on a 1965 base of 50 and that use the market values of all the stocks listed on the New York Stock Exchange. The NYSE series is weighted according to each stock's market value so that the stocks of large companies have a large impact on the index.

NASDAQ Series—A series of seven price indicators calculated using all of the domestic over-the-counter stocks on NASDAQ. Each series is calculated using market value weights with a base of 100 in 1971.

Wilshire 5000 Equity Index—A market value weighted index comprised of all the stocks on the New York Stock Exchange and the American Stock Exchange and the most active stocks on the over-the-counter market.

Nikkei–Dow Jones Average—A price weighted index that includes the prices of 225 stocks traded on the Tokyo Stock Exchange.

have all been sold to individual investors with promises of big profits. If someone telephones to inform you of a great investment that doesn't make sense to you, request written material or tell the caller you aren't interested. You are better off keeping your money in insured certificates of deposit, despite their relatively low yield, than risking your savings on an investment you don't understand.

Check with the NASD before doing business with a stockbroker. The National Association of Securities Dealers (NASD) is a nongovernmental organization of over-the-counter (OTC) dealers and brokers that establishes and enforces legal and ethical standards of conduct among its members. The NASD maintains a record of final and pending disciplinary actions against members and associated persons (including stockbrokers), which is made available at no charge to investors. The NASD may be reached with a toll-free call to (800) 289–9999.

Consider all the costs you will be required to pay when you select a custodian for your IRA. IRAs can involve several types of expenses. Many financial institutions charge an initial fee to establish your IRA and another fee to terminate or transfer it. Other institutions charge an annual maintenance fee that is separate from and in addition to charges that may be applied against the investment. Banks, savings-and-loan associations, and credit unions often do not levy any fees. Brokerage firms frequently levy all of the above charges. Mutual funds differ in the fees they charge. Some have no setup or annual fee, while others have one or the other. Mutual funds often have a termination fee in the event that you decide to transfer the IRA to a different institution. Don't forget to consider annual expenses and any sales fee when you evaluate a mutual fund. Ask each potential custodian to explain any charges you may be required to pay.

Avoid penny stocks. Low-priced stocks (also called *penny stocks*) are appealing because you can't lose much money by owning them. If you purchase 1,000 shares of a 50-cent stock, you can't lose more than the $500 you invest. On the other hand, $500 represents 100 percent of your investment. Penny stocks sell at a low price because investors don't believe the shares are worth much. To your dismay, you are likely to discover that the stocks are worth even less than you paid. Many penny stocks have no market other than that created and maintained by the firms that underwrite them, promote them, and establish the price of them. A wide spread often exists between the price at which the dealer sells the stock and the price at which the same dealer will purchase the stock. As the firm making a market in penny stocks transfers its energies to different securities (or is closed down by government authorities), you may discover the securities you purchased have little value to other investors.

If an investment seems too good to be true, it probably is. Whenever an investment is promoted as a sure thing, or the return you are promised is substantially higher than the returns available on comparable investments, either ask for more information or simply walk away. Unusually high rates of return are normally available only on investments that entail substantial risk. For example, junk bonds provide current returns that are higher than U.S. Treasury bills because owners of junk bonds stand a greater chance of not being paid. If an investment is being pitched on the basis of an unusually high return you can be certain that ownership entails great risk or the promoter is selling a bill of goods. Don't become greedy and reach for a high return unless you understand the potential consequences.

Consider AMT municipal bonds if you invest in tax-exempt bonds. Some municipal bonds pay interest that is subject to the federal alternative minimum tax (AMT). This tax is designed to make certain that individuals who enjoy substantial tax preferences are required to pay at least a minimum amount of tax. Most individual taxpayers are not subject to the alternative minimum tax. Municipal bonds that pay interest subject to the AMT provide relatively high yields because they are less desirable to investors who may be required to pay the alternative minimum tax. If you are not subject to this tax, you can pick up additional tax-exempt income by purchasing AMT bonds. The additional yield won't be substantial, but you may be able to earn an additional .1 or .15 of a percent annually. Your broker will be able to determine which bonds pay interest that is subject to the alternative minimum tax.

Buy U.S. Savings Bonds to pay for your children's college education. Series EE U.S. Savings Bonds purchased after December 31, 1989, pay interest that may be exempt from federal taxes if the proceeds are used to pay tuition and fees (after adjusting for net of grants or scholarships) at institutions of higher learning. Parents filing a joint tax return with a modified adjusted gross income of up to $60,000 can take full advantage of the tax exemption. Tax benefits are phased out on modified adjusted gross incomes from $60,000 to

$90,000. Comparable limitations for single individuals range from $40,000 to $55,000. (These limitations, which are indexed annually for inflation, were applicable for 1994.) To qualify for the exemption, Savings Bonds must be registered in the names of one or both parents who must be at least twenty-four years of age at the time the bonds are purchased. Series EE Savings Bonds may be purchased in person or by mail through most banks and savings institutions. For additional information request the free publications *The Savings Bonds Question and Answer Book* and *publication SBD-1964* from the Office of Public Affairs, U.S. Savings Bonds Division, Washington, DC 20226.

Purchase Treasury securities directly and save a sales fee. Treasury securities can be purchased in two ways: directly from the Treasury or indirectly through a brokerage company or commercial bank. Choose the latter route and you will pay a one-time fee of $30 to $50. Direct purchase of Treasuries does not entail any fees, which means a savings for you. Short-term Treasury securities (called *Treasury bills*) with 13-week and 26-week maturities (the date on which the face value is paid to the owner) are auctioned each Monday. Treasuries with one-year maturities are offered monthly. You can also directly purchase Treasury securities with maturities longer than one year. Keep in mind that only *newly issued* Treasury securities can be purchased directly; existing Treasury securities (those issued previously and currently being traded among investors) can only be acquired in the secondary market through a brokerage firm or commercial bank. Also note that the direct-purchase route should only be utilized when you intend to keep the securities to maturity. Direct purchase of Treasury securities is relatively uncomplicated, and directions are available from the Federal Reserve, the agency that sells the securities for the U.S. Treasury.

Beware of frequent switching of mutual funds. Every individual's investment portfolio requires occasional fine tuning. A change in either your financial goals or risk profile means you should consider rearranging your investments. Replacing investments you already own, however, is in some respects similar to moving to a new home; the change may cost you a lot of money. The expense of switching investments can be particularly costly when you switch among mutual funds that charge sales and redemption fees. Keep in mind that a broker who recommends that you switch mutual funds stands to benefit financially from the switch, because a new sales fee will be generated. If you expect occasionally to switch mutual funds, invest your money with an organization that sponsors a family of funds that permits switches at minimal cost to you.

Don't waste your money on get-rich-quick books. Every investment season has its schemers ready to explain how even a knucklehead can get rich quick. Real estate prices boom and a thousand books appear on how to get rich with no money down in real estate. Stock indexes hit new highs and publishers churn out books on how to become wealthy by investing according to somebody's investment formula. Authors offer to show you how to prosper from the approaching depression, the coming currency crisis, World War III, or an invasion of giant termites. Ask yourself why these individuals are willing to part with such valuable information. Save your money by avoiding the books, even if they become best sellers. If you want to learn about investments, find some basic books that explain the risks and returns of various types of investments.

Consider short- and intermediate-term U. S. Treasury securities as alternatives to certificates of deposit. Certificates of deposit (CDs) have their advantages. They are safe and convenient, two very important features. Sometimes, though, they offer relatively low yields compared to the returns available from U.S. Treasury securities. Payment of principal and interest on Treasuries is guaranteed by the U.S. government, which makes these securities just as safe as certificates of deposit. Interest on U.S. Treasury securities is exempt from state and local taxes. Although treasuries can vary in market value, especially when the maturities are long, those maturing in a year or less experience only minor fluctuations in market value. U.S. Treasury securities can be purchased through a commercial bank or brokerage firm for a nominal commission.

Don't allow tax considerations to outweigh common sense. Some individuals seem willing to go to any extreme to minimize the taxes they pay, including placing their funds in investments that produce *lower* after-tax returns than could be earned from taxable investments. Some tax-saving ideas make sense and some don't. Don't fall for investment ideas that promise great tax savings if you will be required to place your funds at great risk. It is irresponsible to refinance your home with a big mortgage in order to invest the proceeds of the loan in a tax-deferred annuity, even though the transaction may produce substantial current tax savings. Likewise, cashing in your life insurance in order to obtain funds to invest in an oil drilling partnership is asking for trouble. Ignore investment advice from individuals you don't know who try to convince you to invest in tax-saving schemes. Avoid as well investing in tax-saving schemes you don't understand. Investments that promise mostly tax savings are generally very risky.

Buy bonds when they are issued instead of in the secondary market. Bonds, like stocks, can be purchased at the time they are issued, or later when investors trade the bonds in the secondary market. Organizations that issue bonds (and stocks) absorb the sales fee at the time of issue, but not on subsequent trades. By purchasing corporate and municipal bonds at the time they are issued, you avoid a sales fee and are assured of paying the same price as all other investors, even those with more money and clout than yourself. Bonds can be tricky to purchase in the secondary market and a small investor often pays a higher price than that paid by investors with more money. Financial institutions that sell new bond issues are required to quote the same price to all buyers. A broker can inform you of upcoming bond issues. The *Wall Street Journal* and major daily newspapers also provide information on bonds issues that will soon be brought to market.

CHAPTER 5

Miscellaneous Money Smarts

Gain control of your finances by putting together a personal budget. Regularly read several money management and consumer magazines. Think before you spend. Consider how long it takes to earn the money you are getting ready to spend. Alternatively, consider the other goods and services you could purchase with the money you are spending.

Don't pay to include your name in a vanity publication.
Don't waste money to have your name included in a "famous persons" publication. Publications such as *Who's Important in Bridge, Big Shots of the Midwest, World Class Hog Farmers*, and *America's Outstanding Barbers* prey on people's need for recognition, even though recognition may not be warranted. Many vanity publications offer to include your name and abbreviated biography in a fancy and overpriced book in anticipation that you will purchase one or more copies of the publication. If you take time to complete and return the application, the publisher is betting that you are likely to want a copy of the finished product to show your friends and relatives, especially your mother-in-law. Virtually no one reads these publications. A college faculty member once nominated *his dog* for inclusion in one of the better-known vanity publications. The dog was accepted!

If you need to make a long-distance telephone call to a business, determine whether the firm has a toll-free number. The *Wall Street Journal* reported that two-thirds of manufacturers have implemented incoming toll-free telephone numbers to facilitate communications with their customers, employees, and suppliers. Gerber, Procter & Gamble, Frito-Lay, Dow, Kraft, Mars, and Campbell Soup Company all have toll-free 800 numbers. So have many other companies, including firms in businesses other than manufacturing. Toll-free lines are often designed for a specific purpose, such as taking orders and facilitating consumer comments. Even if the line is not intended for the kind of call you are placing, try calling the toll-free number, then request that your call be redirected to the appropriate person or department. To determine if the company you wish to contact has a toll-free number, call toll-free information at (800) 555–1212. Manufacturers frequently print toll-free telephone numbers on products, and directories of toll-free numbers are available from several publishers. Be aware that many toll-free numbers are unlisted and, thus, unavailable from information.

Be wary of making long distance calls from a pay telephone. Partial deregulation of the telephone industry has opened the long-distance telephone business both to bargains and rip-offs. One potential trouble spot for consumers is the use of pay telephones. Owners of restaurants, hotels, or other businesses can now choose their long-distance providers. Some long-distance services charge prices much higher than you pay at home and offer business owners increased profit for using their services. Owners of businesses normally don't make long distance calls on their pay phones, so why should they care what calls cost? Many customers who make long distance calls are passing through and won't discover they have been overcharged until the bill arrives at their home the following month. Ask the operator about the toll charge before you make a call to be certain you won't get ripped off. Alternatively, ask to be connected with your regular long-distance company. If you get stonewalled, make a toll-free call to AT&T (800–225–5288), MCI (800–674–7000), or Sprint (800–674–8000).

Don't make telephone calls from your hotel or motel room until you determine the charge. A telephone call from a hotel or motel room often turns out to be one of life's biggest rip-offs. Hotels and motels sometimes charge their own customers exorbitant amounts to make both local and

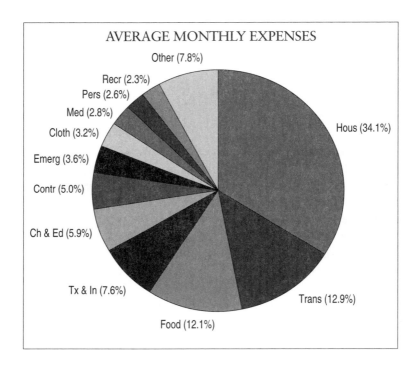

AVERAGE MONTHLY EXPENSES

Other (7.8%)

Recr (2.3%)

Pers (2.6%)

Med (2.8%)

Cloth (3.2%)

Emerg (3.6%)

Contr (5.0%)

Ch & Ed (5.9%)

Tx & In (7.6%)

Food (12.1%)

Trans (12.9%)

Hous (34.1%)

toll calls. You may end up paying 50 to 75 cents or even more to make a local telephone call when you expect to pay 25 cents! You are also likely to overpay for long distance calls made from your room. No restrictions are imposed on the amount hotels or motels charge guests who make long distance telephone calls from their rooms. You may not even receive discounts for late-night or weekend calls. Make certain you understand the charges *before you make either local or long distance telephone calls from your room.* Call the front office and ask about the schedule of charges for telephone calls. If you fail to learn beforehand how much will be charged, you won't discover the bad news until you check out of the hotel. Walk to the lobby and use a pay telephone. Once there, check the cost of a long distance call in case the hotel has service with a high-cost carrier.

Make a free telephone call for free travel information. Most state visitor information bureaus maintain a toll-free telephone number for travelers who desire information about towns, parks, and popular attractions. Detailed state maps and informative brochures can be acquired at no cost to you. Obtain the telephone number of the tourist bureau of a particular state by calling toll-free information at (800) 555–1212. Try to call at least a month or more prior to the time you will need the material as it generally takes this long to receive the requested information. Most tourist bureaus are able to provide information on camping and lodging facilities in select towns and regions. Make a list of the information you need before you place the call so that you won't forget anything.

Generally pass up a maintenance warranty unless you expect to be a heavy user of what you purchase. Manufacturers and retailers frequently offer optional maintenance warranties for durable goods. Expect the salesperson who sells you a washing machine, automobile, computer, or stereo system to ask if you wish to purchase a maintenance contract at added cost. If the item already includes a limited warranty—say for the first 90 days or the first year—the optional warranty will specify a period beyond the expiration of the standard warranty. The manufacturer's or retailer's charge for a maintenance contract is computed for the average user. The charge typically includes a profit for the company that offers the warranty plus a commission for the salesperson who sells it to you, making the extended warranty a bad buy if you anticipate being a light user of the product. Washing four or five loads of clothes per week produces relatively few maintenance problems. The same reasoning applies to a computer, a stereo, and a vehicle. An extended vehicle warranty is likely to be a bad buy for weekend drivers.

Subscribe to (and read) *Consumer Reports.* Suppose your twenty-year-old washing machine is about to go to washing machine heaven, and you have decided to shop for a replacement. Which of the numerous makes and models should you buy, and how much should you expect to pay? Different brands and models of washing machines have different repair histories, consume different amounts of energy, and have different controls. Maybe you have observed increasing numbers of multi-legged pests walking through your kitchen and are ready to call a pest control company. How do you determine which company offers the best service and guarantee? You can expect to encounter these types of problems throughout your life. You can't get your money's worth if you don't know the facts, and you can't know all the facts about all the products you need to purchase. So where can you obtain the facts? *Consumer Reports* is probably the single best popular source of product evaluations. One of the few publications that does not accept paid advertising, *Consumer Reports* provides unbiased evaluations about product quality and value. The publication evaluates air conditioners, automobiles, life insurance, movies, televisions, and hundreds of other items you regularly buy or are likely to need. With no advertisers to offend, the consumer products testing organization is unafraid to point out negatives of any product it tests.

Buy rechargeable batteries and a battery charger. If you and other family members, especially your children, are heavy users of battery-powered items—radios, cassette players, toys, flashlights, smoke detectors, clocks, and so forth—substantial savings can be gained by substituting nickel-cadmium rechargeable batteries for regular, heavy duty, or alkaline throwaways. Rechargeable batteries have a higher initial cost compared to throwaways, but they can be used over and over again, so that the initial expense is spread over many uses. Battery chargers are relatively inexpensive ($15 to $25); it shouldn't take long to recover your initial outlay for a charger and rechargeable batteries. Be forewarned that fully charged rechargeable batteries do not last as long as new alkaline batteries. You probably won't want to use rechargeables in a flashlight you will be taking on an extended camping trip.

Eat out at a discount. Try to steer your eating companions to a restaurant where you can eat at a discount. The restaurant business, including the fast-food segment, is very competitive. Restaurants want your business so badly that many regularly offer various discounts. Newspapers feature restaurant discount coupons offering 20 percent, 25 percent, or even 50 percent off. Other coupons provide one free meal for each meal purchased. Some restaurants promote business with family nights that allow kids eat to free. Some even permit two children to eat free with each paying adult. You can't eat this cheaply at home! You can likewise join a restaurant club or purchase one of the many discount coupon books that are regularly sold by schools or charitable organizations. Restaurant clubs often feature half-price meals or one free meal for each meal purchased. Restaurant owners hope to attract new customers who will become regular patrons. Coupon books are designed to bring in extra business by offering discounts to individuals who would otherwise stay at home or go elsewhere.

Earn college credits outside college. Your child may be able to accelerate college graduation by earning college credits while in high school, or through tests administered before or after entering college. Good high school students who are fortunate enough to live near a college may be able to enroll in college courses prior to their high school graduation. Credits for college courses successfully completed during a high school student's junior or senior year count toward a college degree. Students can also earn college credits in math, English, history, and many other academic areas by passing certain standardized tests before entering college or, sometimes, during college. For information concerning these tests, check with the dean of students or admissions department of the college your child will be attending. Each college establishes its own requirements for accepting credits earned via testing. Gather information on the tests well in advance, because it is best to take these examinations before entering college. Scores you receive may also influence the college you choose to attend.

Take extra college courses. Colleges often permit their regular students to take extra courses at a reduced charge or at no extra charge. For example, a college might levy tuition on a per-credit-hour basis up to a specified number of credit hours. Beyond this point the student is considered a full-timer, and tuition remains unchanged, regardless of how many additional credit hours are carried; five courses cost no more than four courses. The tuition policy for overloads varies among colleges, so read the catalog or contact the registrar of the particular college in which you are interested. Keep in mind that it doesn't pay to have your child enroll in additional courses if the extra load is likely to result in lower grades.

Check on the availability of a college co-op program. An increasing number of colleges offer cooperative education programs in which students work full time, usually during alternate quarters or semesters, including summers. Co-op programs allow students to earn money that helps to pay for their education while they gain the work experience needed to find employment following graduation (sometimes with the same firms for which they worked in the co-op programs). With the intense competition for good jobs, employers increasingly search for students with job experience. If you think this sounds like a good idea, make certain that a college has an active co-op program before your son or daughter enrolls. Inquire about the participating companies and the number of students involved. Remember, most companies restrict participation to students with particular majors. It is best to begin the program as early as possible, usually during the first term of the junior year.

Draw names for Christmas gifts. Instead of giving every extended family member a modest gift, draw names and have each family member give and receive a single useful gift. Enjoy whatever bounty you can afford with members of your immediate family. After all, it can be depressing to have only a couple of gifts under the Christmas tree. With numerous brothers, sisters, aunts, uncles, cousins, nephews, and nieces, however, you will save yourself a lot of expense and stress by drawing names. You may want to establish a limit on the cost of presents to be given so that hard feelings don't develop over presents of widely varying values.

Take your lunch to work. Regularly taking your lunch to work is an easy way to save substantial amounts of money over the course of a year. Suppose you normally spend $4.95 for lunch at a restaurant, versus $1.50 for a lunch made at home and taken to work. Assuming you work five days a week for 48 weeks a year, you will save $3.45 for 240 days, or $828.00 annually. Not only that, you will save on tips and taxes, accomplish more, be more rested for the afternoon, and impress the boss with your work ethic and common sense. The variety of meals you can tote is substantially expanded if you have access to a small refrigerator and microwave at your workplace. If these aren't currently available, see if your employer will spring for the two inexpensive appliances. If this doesn't work, ask fellow employees who frequently bring lunches if they would be interested in contributing to the purchase of these items. Even if you have to buy the appliances yourself, it is a good investment that should pay for itself in three months. Your savings are all tax-free!

Complain if you feel you have been ripped off. Like every other consumer, you have probably been overcharged, shortchanged, purchased spoiled food, and bought things that didn't work. Many people get ripped off but don't do anything about it, either because it is too much trouble or they believe nothing will happen to remedy the situation. You actually do businesses a favor when you complain about their poor service or faulty products. Businesses need to know if a problem exists, or managers will assume customers are satisfied. With an increased emphasis on quality control, most companies want to know when things aren't right. Many businesses support a toll-free telephone service so consumers can contact the firm with questions and comments. To learn who to contact and the best way to voice a complaint, send for a free copy of *Consumer's Resource Handbook* by writing: Office of Consumer Affairs, Department of Health and Human Services, 1620 L Street NW, Suite 700, Washington, DC 20036 (202–634–4140). This publication provides consumer tips, a sample complaint letter, and addresses and contact persons for many companies and state consumer organizations.

Make consecutive credit card telephone calls from a hotel room. You can often save the hotel surcharge on credit card telephone calls if you make consecutive calls (*i.e.*, don't hang up between calls). Hotels frequently charge up to $2 for each credit card call from your room. By stringing together as many calls as possible without hanging up you can often save surcharges on all calls that follow the initial call. The secret is to press the pound key (#) instead of hanging up when you finish a conversation. The pound key terminates a call and allows you to dial another number without entering your credit card identification.

Sell your old tires. Like most consumers, you probably give your old tires to the dealer when you purchase new tires.

Dealers typically don't pay anything for the old tires and would just as soon that you cart them away. A better idea may be to take the old tires with you and advertise them for sale. Of course, you can't spend much for advertising because the tires aren't worth much. Try a shopping guide that offers free classified advertisements for items selling below a certain price, or post some notices at the laundromat. Don't ask too high a price—perhaps $25 a pair, or even $10 per tire. Include the brand, size, and price in your advertisement. This assumes, of course, that you haven't worn the tires to the point that the steel belts are visible. If so, leave the tires with the dealer and consider yourself lucky.

Fax local correspondence. Have you ever thought how unfair it is that you have to pay the same postage for a letter to someone several blocks away as for a letter to someone living a thousand miles away? A telephone call to these individuals doesn't cost the same, so why should a letter? Technology now allows you to beat this system by sending local correspondence via your no-cost local telephone system. You will not only save the money for first class postage, but your message will arrive sooner when you use the fax. Fax machines are rapidly declining in price. A high-speed fax/modem for your computer now costs only about $100. If local calls are free then local faxes are free, so you may as well take advantage of this bargain.

Have your children complete their first two years of college at a community college. Community colleges generally offer a bargain education compared to the cost of four-year public and, especially, private institutions of higher learning. The lower cost doesn't mean your children will receive an inferior education. Community colleges hire faculty members to teach, not to conduct and publish research. This specialization allows community colleges to direct more of their budgets toward teaching faculty. Research certainly benefits faculty members who teach graduate courses and upper-level undergraduate courses, but it has little relevance for instructors who teach freshmen and sophomores. Upon completion of two years of college work and receipt of an associate's degree, students can transfer to a four-year college to finish a bachelor's degree. This allows the students to earn a more prestigious degree at a substantially reduced cost.

Stay away from lotteries. If fools and their money soon part, then lotteries are definitely for fools. Buying a lottery ticket is one of the world's worst wagers. It's worse than betting the horses, playing the slots, or rolling the dice. Most lotteries pay winners no more than 50 percent of the amount bet. In other words, over time lottery players have only about half their money returned. For every dollar bet on a lottery, approximately 10 cents is used to cover expenses for operating the lottery, 5 cents reimburses the outlets that sell tickets, and 35 cents goes to some worthy cause such as education. The remaining 50 cents is paid to lottery winners, who must pay income taxes on their winnings. Such a meager return makes lotteries a poor gamble, regardless of the type of game you enter. Do yourself a favor and give your favorite charity the money you would normally use to purchase lottery tickets. At least you will benefit from a tax deduction.

Take advantage of fringe benefits offered by your employer. Employers often offer worthwhile fringe benefits to full-time employees. For example, many employers offer 401(k) plans that save pretax dollars (*i.e.,* contributions reduce your gross income and the income taxes you pay on this income) in a retirement account. Some employers even match your contributions up to a certain percentage of your salary. Many employers also offer flexible spending accounts for medical and child care expenses. Again, you are able to put aside pretax dollars. Employers sometimes pick up a portion of health insurance and life insurance premiums. Both types of insurance are probably a good deal if you need either coverage. Inquire about the fringe benefits your employer offers and consider taking advantage of them. Don't miss potential benefits offered by your employer because of inertia on your part.

Turn your hobby into a sideline business. You may be pursuing some activity that can be turned into a part-time business enterprise. Perhaps you make designer T-shirts for family and friends. Maybe you enjoy woodworking or making stained glass pieces. Or you may collect stamps, coins, or baseball cards. Why not put your knowledge and interest into a business? Making a sideline business from a hobby allows you to supplement your regular income while claiming certain tax benefits. For example, you may be able to deduct expenses you incur for transportation and equipment. Likewise, you may be able to hire members of your family and deduct payments to them. You may be eligible for a deduction for home office expenses, including a portion of the cost of utilities, maintenance, and insurance. Keep in mind that you must convince tax authorities that you have a profit motive and, in general, show a profit in three out of five years. Do not try to claim you are in the business of growing couch potatoes!

Purge your Christmas gift and card lists. Most people suffer from inertia, especially when a holiday ritual is involved. They continue to trade Christmas gifts or cards with former neighbors, co-workers, or friends long after the gesture has become virtually meaningless. Dropping individuals from your list isn't necessarily cruel; your friends might prefer to do the same, but your cards or gifts force them to respond in kind. Think about purging your Christmas list of individuals who either don't respond or who don't include a written note in their cards. Consider as well whether it is time to quit giving gifts to nieces or nephews who are now grown and on their own. The key is to evaluate your card and gift lists immediately after the current Christmas season when the whole process (and headaches) of card sending and gift buying is fresh in your mind.

Make and bake Christmas presents. Are you good at baking cakes, pies, cookies, or at painting shirts, knitting socks, or woodworking? How about taking photographs or making pottery? All these items make terrific gifts that recipients will appreciate much more than items you purchase. Wouldn't you rather receive a freshly made pecan pie than another gaudy tie that will end up on the back of your tie rack? Homemade gifts save considerable amounts of money compared to the cost of store-bought items. You can reduce time and expense by making things in quantity. Bake several cakes at one time and save on the energy required to bake and to clean dirty pots and pans. If time runs short and you are unable to complete gifts for all the people on your list, think about giving certificates stating that the item will be forthcoming.

AVERAGE MONTHLY COST OF FOOD AT HOME
FOR FOOD PLANS AT FOUR COST LEVELS, 1994

Family Size	Thrifty	Low-cost	Moderate	Liberal
Individuals				
Male (age 20–50)	$107.80	$137.70	$173.00	$209.60
Male (51 and over)	97.50	131.50	162.40	194.60
Female (age 20–50)	97.00	121.50	147.70	188.90
Female (51 and over)	95.80	117.70	145.80	174.40
Families				
Family of 2 (ages 20–50)	225.30	285.10	352.80	438.40
Family of 2 (51 and over)	212.60	274.10	339.00	405.90
Family of 4				
Children ages 1–5	328.40	410.70	502.70	617.80
Children ages 6–11	376.30	482.70	604.10	727.00

Source: Agricultural Research Service, U.S. Department of Agriculture, *USDA Family Food Plans (Oct. 1994)*

Order water with a restaurant meal. Soft drinks, tea, and coffee are among the most overpriced items offered by restaurants. How much does it cost to make a glass of ice tea that sells for $1.00? Fast food restaurants often offer sandwiches at bargain prices in anticipation that customers will also order overpriced drinks and fries that cost almost as much as the sandwich. Upscale restaurants charge even more for the drinks they serve, although drink prices generally amount to a lower proportion of the total price of the meals. Is $1.50 a fair price for a cup of coffee? The best deal is to ask for water and skip overpriced drinks. If you want a little flavor, ask for a lemon wedge.

Generally avoid rent-to-own stores. "Rent to own" sounds like a good method for acquiring a major appliance or a set of bedroom furniture. Make rental payments for the required number of months and you become the owner. How can you lose? You can lose if the rent-to-own firm charges prices that are much higher than you would otherwise pay, shopping carefully and buying the items outright, or even borrowing a portion of the purchase price. Rent-to-own firms often charge very high prices for their goods. Before acquiring a new rent-to-own television (or any other item), compare the required rental payments with the payments necessary to buy a comparable television at several different retailers. Examine newspaper advertisements to locate the lowest price, and then inquire about the payments that would be required over a period equivalent to that offered by the rent-to-own store. Also determine if a delivery charge is required. If so, incorporate the charge into your comparison.

Buy the basics. Basic items tend to be easy for manufacturers to duplicate so that competition keeps prices low. For example, basic sweatshirts are manufactured by many companies, distributed through a large number of stores, and sold mostly on the basis of price. Fancy sweatshirts, because they are featured by their manufacturer's name, can be sold at a higher price. Likewise, basic cereals without added fruits, marshmallows, and other special ingredients are sold at relatively low prices, because several virtually identical brands are available for consumers to choose. It is most economical to purchase the basic version of a product and, if desired, add whatever extras you desire. If you prefer dry cereal with raisins, buy a package of raisins to mix with a basic dry cereal. Buy a plain sweatshirt and stitch or iron on attractive decorations. Purchase plain pasta and add the cheese and spices that come packaged at greater cost in a boxed dinner. The possibilities are endless, but the result is the same; you will save money by buying the basics.

Consider a prepaid telephone calling card for making long-distance calls away from home. Numerous firms, including the major long-distance carriers AT&T, MCI, and Sprint, offer prepaid telephone calling cards. These cards allow substantial savings when making long distance calls away from home, especially if the calls are of short duration and occur mostly during business hours. Alhough prepayment is a disadvantage, other features more than compensate. Rates remain the same using prepaid cards regardless of the day or time a call is made. If most calls occur during weekday business hours significant savings can result. Prepaid cards do not carry the surcharge that regular telephone calling cards do. Per-minute charges on prepaid cards vary substantially by seller, however, and are likely to vary depending on the value of the card you purchase (higher value cards offer cheaper rates per minute), so it is worthwhile to shop for the best price. Cards are usually sold in denominations of $5, $10, and $20. If you make frequent but relatively short calls at peak times, a prepaid telephone calling card should be one of your travel companions.

Avoid vacation time-shares. Consider time-shares of vacation properties (also called *interval ownership*) a bad deal. Time-shares allow use of a property for a particular period of time, usually a week. They often come with the added benefit of being tradable for a week at an affiliated property. Use may be restricted to a particular week of the year or to certain months, depending on seasonal demand for the property. The price you pay includes the high costs of marketing such a property to fifty buyers (two weeks are usually set aside for maintenance), a price too high for the benefits you receive. Carefully evaluate the costs, including the initial outlay and annual maintenance fees, and compare the total to what you would pay to vacation at a nice resort at the regular daily or weekly fee. A sales presentation for a time-share will probably claim an easy resale of your ownership interval to someone else. In truth, these ownership periods are often impossible to unload at anywhere near the price you paid. If you attend a sale presentation for a time-share, look bored, don't ask questions, don't sign anything, collect your prize, and get out as quickly as possible.

Keep a thermos beside your coffeemaker. This is a simple idea that can save you money while it keeps your coffee tasting better. Instead of leaving coffee for several hours (or perhaps all day) in your coffeemaker, pour freshly-made coffee into a nearby thermos and turn off the coffeemaker. You will save hundreds of watts of electricity, and the thermos will keep the coffee warm and tasting fresh-brewed. Most coffeemakers cause coffee to become bitter after a relatively short warming period. Coffee that eventually becomes too cool in the thermos can be reheated in your microwave.

Complete and send refunds immediately. How many times have you purchased an item in order to qualify for a refund and then forgotten to complete or lost the refund form? Avoid both these possibilities by completing and mailing the refund form immediately after purchasing the qualifying item. Leave the required refund form(s) on the counter when you leave home to do your shopping. Take care of the business at hand immediately on your return.

Pass on the snacks. Prepackaged snacks are expensive and often nutritionally bankrupt. Buying snacks wastes your money and consuming snacks wastes your body. Keep a bowl of chilled celery, carrots, and radishes on the top shelf of the refrigerator to satisfy occasional hunger pangs. Have fruits, such as apples and oranges, handy. If you have difficulty maintaining your weight and cholesterol level at the same time your budget is out of balance, kill two birds with one stone and pass up that candy bar or package of snack crackers. Once you are able to break the habit, the rest is easy.

Cook extra helpings of food to freeze and eat later. The next time you concoct yet another great casserole or some time-consuming dish, make sure you cook up extra helpings to freeze and consume another day. You may normally cook more than you need for a single meal, but next time buy sufficient ingredients to cook enough for several additional meals. Having ready-made meals available in the freezer means that when your family members are hungry and you lack the time or energy to cook, you won't have to rely on TV dinners or boxed meals that tend to be more expensive, less nutritious, and not as tasty as your own cooking.

Plant a garden. If you want some low-cost, high-nutrition food, grow your own. It takes time and effort, of course. You have to fight the insects, the elements, and the neighborhood pets, but the return on your investment is high. Concentrate your efforts on vegetables that bring the highest prices at the store and the highest yields in a garden.

Choose vegetables based on your climate and the space you have available. If thinking about the toil and trouble of a garden brings on a headache, consider the time you probably devote to your yard, even though you can't eat the grass. Wouldn't it be nice to stroll to the back yard and pick some tasty fresh tomatoes to replace the sawdust variety from the supermarket that sometimes sell for over $1.00 per pound? How about growing your own peppers, broccoli, eggplant, and green beans? You will enjoy both savings and a sense of accomplishment.

Delay your retirement. Delaying your retirement by several years can make a dramatic difference in the standard of living you will enjoy during your retirement years. Waiting a couple of extra years to retire will allow you to make extra contributions to your retirement fund, which will increase the annual income the fund provides after you drop out of the labor force. Retiring at a slightly older age will also allow you to receive an increased annual retirement income. Consider what valuable fringe benefits are likely to be terminated at your retirement. For example, you will be required to pick up the expense of medical insurance premiums if you retire when you are too young to qualify for Medicare. Your employer may pay premiums for life insurance and disability income insurance that you will have to pay following retirement. One major factor in your decision about when to retire, of course, is how much you enjoy your employment. If you enjoy what you are doing, stick with it a couple of more years.

If you have kids, eat out where the kids eat free. Many restaurants offer free meals to kids who are accompanied by a paying adult. In fact, some restaurants provide free meals for up to two children with one paying adult. It's hard to beat that, even by cooking at home. Although restrictions vary, most restaurants impose an age limit and specify one specific night each week. For example, Shoneys, a restaurant chain headquartered in Nashville, Tennessee, allows two kids (12 and under) to eat free on Wednesday nights with the purchase of each adult entrée. Most TGI Friday's offer free meals for two kids (12 and under) with each adult entrée on Monday nights. Fuddrucker locations often offer free meals for kids Monday through Thursday. Telephone a specific restaurant if you are in doubt. Don't forget to inquire about the age limit, as well as restrictions regarding the night of the week. Once you determine the magic nights, plan frequent evenings out without fretting about the cost. Free eats for kids is especially valuable for working single parents.

Sell or donate unused items. If your vehicles remain parked in the elements because your garage is piled with multiple layers of junk, or if there isn't room in your attic for one additional box, it is time to clean house and put some spare change in your pocket with a garage sale. Everything, no matter how useless and dated, seems to have value for someone. Conduct an inspection of your garage, attic, and basement and mark the items you haven't needed for a year or longer. Old chairs, clothes, golf clubs, fishing gear, picture frames, tables, garden tools, lamps, and other items of a former life are fair game for a garage sale. Drag it all out and let the bargain hunters pay you for carrying away your junk. Throw what you can't sell into the trunk of your car, transport it to a charitable organization (some organizations will pick up if you call), and obtain a receipt for a tax deduction. You have gained space and some spending money at the same time.

Eat meatless meals. Save on your food bills by increasing the number of meatless meals you eat. You will also save on the calories, fat, and cholesterol. Meat tends to be a relatively expensive source of the nutrients your body requires. It also contains some things your body is better off without. Both your pocketbook and your body will be in better shape if you substitute increased amounts of vegetables and fruits for the meats you normally consume. Have a salad or a bowl of soup in place of a hamburger and french fries for lunch. For dinner, substitute a couple of ears of corn and green beans or a rice-and-bean dish for pork chops. Eliminate bacon and sausage from breakfast. It won't be long before less meat will become a money-saving habit.

Cancel subscriptions to magazines you don't have time to read. Like many people, you probably subscribe to more magazines than you and other family members have time to read. You have good intentions, but stacks of unread or partially-read magazines grow ever taller beside your bed. If this describes your situation, why not save money and make it easier to vacuum the bedroom by terminating at least some of the subscriptions. If one of the magazines periodically publishes a survey or story on a subject in which you are interested, read the magazine in the library. Consider sharing magazine subscriptions with a friend who has similar interests. Subscribe to *Sports Illustrated* and have your friend subscribe to *Newsweek*.

Cancel memberships to organizations in which you are no longer active. Inertia and loyalty to organizations that years ago lost your interest and participation may result in substantial outlays as you renew annual memberships. Perhaps you have long belonged to a fraternal organization that once occupied an important place in your social life, but which now you only infrequently visit. Maybe you belong to several environmental organizations that you joined many years ago as a young activist. Do you belong to a country club you seldom use? Memberships nearly always involve annual fees, sometimes substantial fees, that could be saved by cancellation. In many instances you may be able to save a lot of money with very little loss or inconvenience. To get started, list the annual membership cost for each of the organizations to which you belong. Then decide on a case-by-case basis which memberships should be retained and which should be canceled.

Substitute potluck meals for dinner parties. Next time it is your turn to entertain, save time and money by asking each of your guests to bring a dish to a potluck supper. You must still clean the house, of course, but it won't be necessary to purchase as much food or spend as many hours preparing a variety of dishes. You also won't need to stick with bland selections to ensure that all the guests can tolerate the fare. At the extreme you may be able to avoid virtually any expenses by supplying only the (nonalcoholic) drinks. A more expensive and, perhaps, more acceptable alternative is to supply the main dish and request that each guest bring a salad or dessert. Regardless of your choice, you will save money and satisfy a social obligation at the same time.

Split a dessert when you eat out. How many times have you ordered dessert after a meal and, after finishing, wished you had passed on the dessert? Not only did it add to your waistline, it also padded your bill. Next time split a dessert with your companion and save both money and calories. Why stuff yourself at extra cost? Desserts are generally expensive compared to the price of a complete meal. Waiters and waitresses are accustomed to customers sharing desserts and can be expected to bring an extra fork or spoon. Both your conscience and your billfold will feel better when you walk out the door.

Patronize theater matinees. Viewing a movie at a theater matinee can shave up to half the price off what you would pay to buy a ticket to see the same movie in the evening. Is it actually worth twice as much to view a new movie in the evening? Although weekday matinees are no longer offered at many theaters, weekend matinees are generally available and are usually less crowded than evening showings. Theaters that offer matinee showings at reduced ticket prices include this information in their newspaper advertising. If no discount is indicated, phone the theater and ask about matinee discounts. If they aren't available, ask why. If enough people call, the theater's management may institute a discount and reduce your cost of entertainment.

Carry your own canned drink into a fast food restaurant. Fast food restaurants sometimes offer main meal items at bargain prices in anticipation that customers will also order high-profit items such as french fries and soft drinks. To take advantage of this system, carry in your own soft drinks and limit your order to the bargain items. Maximize savings by purchasing canned soft drinks by the case when they are on sale. It is not unusual to be able to purchase name-brand soft drinks for $4.99 per case, or 21 cents per can. If you locate soft drinks on sale at $3.99 per case, as is sometimes possible, the unit cost is only 17 cents per can. Carry one of these into a fast food restaurant and substitute your 21- cent drink for the restaurant's 99-cent offering. You and a spouse or friend can save $1.60 per visit with no pain and no strain. Pull this off twice a week and you save $160 annually. If you feel conspicuous carrying a couple of cans of Coke or Pepsi into the restaurant, hide the cans in a purse or wrap them in a newspaper. If the drinks are warm, ask for a glass of ice water and pour out the water. Many fast food restaurants have drink bars where you can get your own ice.

Invite friends for dessert rather than dinner. Next time you are thinking about inviting friends to your estate for an elaborate dinner, consider having them instead for a dessert. Bake a cake or pie (or both), buy some ice cream, brew a pot of coffee, and you are set for the evening. The preparation time, cleanup time, and expense of a dessert will be considerably less than for a full-blown dinner, and your guests will probably appreciate it just as much. Choosing to provide only a dessert will also give you a couple of extra hours to clean the house before your guests arrive. This is no small benefit!

CHAPTER 6

Money Management
Money Smarts

Good money management requires time and effort but can pay of in consistent savings and additional income. Shop for the best deals and don't become married to a single financial institution. It is to your financial advantage to delay payments you must make as long as possible so long as you are not penalized. Save postage and check charges by choosing automatic payment plans.

Purchase checks from a source other than your bank. Contrary to popular belief, perfectly acceptable and attractive checks are available from sources other than the bank handling your checking account. Buying checks from a bank or savings-and-loan association is convenient, but generally expensive. Outside sources regularly charge $4.95 for 200 checks that are identical to those you would purchase from your bank. Current, Inc. (800–533–3973), a company that sells a variety of paper goods including personalized checks, has been in the mail order business for many years. The company offers a wide variety of check designs, including four with pictures of Elvis. How good can it get!

Pay most of your bills as late as possible without incurring a penalty. Have you noticed that the insurance company, local taxing authority, utility, and nearly everyone else sends bills weeks or even months before payment is due? This gives you time to get sufficient funds together to be able to pay the bill, of course. Early billing also makes it more likely that the institution doing the billing will get its hands on your money earlier. Individuals who want to make certain they won't misplace their bills, or simply want to get them out of the way, often pay invoices as they are received, even when the bills arrive weeks or months ahead of the payment date. Paying bills early, especially bills involving relatively large amounts of money, may make for a more orderly life, but it doesn't make good economic sense. The longer funds are under your control, the longer money can be put to work earning a return for you rather than someone else.

Consider paying small bills ahead of time. Although paying large bills as late as possible usually makes sense, some regular bills may involve such small amounts of money that paying ahead saves more in postage than it costs in lost income. Suppose your newspaper carrier bills you $9.50 each month. Is it better to mail the carrier a check for $9.50 each month or does it make financial sense to save postage by paying two or three months at a time? Suppose you receive the January bill for $9.50 and are considering whether to pay for the months of February and March at the same time. Paying for three months would save two envelopes, two checks, and two first class stamps, say about 72 cents. On the negative side, you lose one month's interest income on $9.50 when you pay ahead on February's subscription, and two month's interest income on another $9.50 when you pay two month's ahead for your March subscription. The amount of lost interest income depends on the return you are able to earn on savings. Assuming a 6-percent annual return, the lost income will amount to:

February payment .06/12 x $9.50 = 4.75 cents
March payment .06/12 x 2 x $9.50 = 9.5 cents

In this example, substantially more is saved in postage (72 cents) than is forgone in interest income (14.25 cents). The same analysis should be used in determining whether to pay ahead for telephone service, cable service, garbage pickup, and so forth. One word of caution: make certain to save the canceled check or obtain a receipt when paying ahead. It is also good practice to write *prepayment* on your check.

Enroll in automatic payment plans. Both postage and time can be saved by allowing companies to debit your bank account for the payment of certain bills. Automatic payment is especially convenient for taking care of recurring charges by the electric company, telephone company, gas company, and mortgage company. Total savings depends on how frequently you use the service. At 32 cents per first class stamp plus a couple of pennies to cover the cost of a check, you should save .34 times 12, or $4.08 annually for each monthly account paid electronically. Paying four accounts in this manner will produce annual savings of $16 plus the time required to write and mail forty-eight checks.

Remain informed of yields offered by money market funds and money market accounts. Money market funds sold by mutual funds and money market accounts offered by banks and savings-and-loan associations are similar investments that often offer substantially different yields. Yields on both investments are influenced by short-term market rates of interest, but not to the same degree. In general, yields on money market mutual funds are more responsive to changes in market interest rates than are yields on money market accounts. Remain alert to yields on both products so that you can quickly move your funds and maximize investment income. Both investments are very liquid (meaning that you enjoy rapid access to the funds, usually by writing a check), so funds can be moved quickly in order to benefit from yield differences.

Don't be afraid to buy certificates of deposit from insured out-of-state financial institutions. If you live in a small community that has only a few noncompetitive financial institutions, or you reside in a region of the country in which interest rates are relatively low, don't be afraid to send your money to an out-of-state FDIC-insured financial institution in order to obtain a higher return. Determine the rates being offered by out-of-state firms by browsing the newspapers at your local library. *Barron's*, a weekly publication available in most libraries, publishes a list of institutions that offer the highest yields on certificates of deposit of various lengths. The same information is available in other financial publications. Many large financial institutions seek out-of-state depositors via toll-free 800 telephone numbers. Ask toll-free information at (800) 555–1212 for the telephone number of a particular institution. Don't send money without first inquiring about the current rates and requirements. For example, ask when interest begins on your deposits and when you will have access to your funds.

Bank your raise. There is no better time to increase the amounts you save than when your income increases. Make a point to put most of an increase in your paycheck into savings. You probably can't expect to set aside your entire raise because added taxes and other expenses will accompany the increase in gross income. Some of the raise, however, should flow through to an increase in net pay (your take-home pay), and a major portion of this increase should be allocated to savings. Banking your raise will allow you to build your savings while you continue to spend the same amount as before the raise.

Pay yourself first. Make a determined effort to put aside at least a small amount of each paycheck. Consistently saving even $40 to $50 a month results in the accumulation of a significant sum of money over a long period of time. Remember, it isn't only the amounts saved that accumulate, but also interest income earned on the savings. If you settle into a pattern of saving a portion of each paycheck, you are likely to discover that it becomes even easier to save additional sums in future years. Saving can become a habit. You will know you have succeeded in a savings program when you reach the point that you feel guilty about not putting aside a portion of each paycheck. If you can live on your current income, then you can almost surely live on just a little bit less. Most people waste enough money between paydays that a modest reduction in spending, if done intelligently, can be accomplished without significant sacrifice.

Establish a personal budget. A personal budget can improve anyone's money management. A personal budget is a system for projecting and recording income and expenditures. Begin by forecasting weekly or monthly income including wages, dividends, interest, and other sources of revenue. This task is relatively easy when the main source of income is a regular salary or wage. Projecting income is more difficult if you earn an hourly wage and face an uncertain work week (perhaps you are employed in the construction business or you operate your own business). Still, you probably have at least a rough idea of the amounts you can expect to earn in the near future. Next, estimate spending for these same periods. This task is made easier if you group expenditures into categories such as groceries, entertainment, housing, insurance, and so forth. Many expenditures, such as rent or house payment and most insurance premiums, remain constant from one period to the next. Projections are initially a learning process, and refinements of weekly or monthly forecasts will be necessary as you encounter estimates that are too high or too low. Maintaining a personal budget requires commitment, but the benefits can be significant. To learn more about how to establish and maintain a personal budget, purchase a copy of *The Guide to Personal Budgeting* by yours truly from The Globe Pequot Press at (800) 243–0495.

Accurately record in your check register deposits and expenditures made by check. A check register is an excellent place to maintain a record of expenditures made by check. Make certain that each entry contains sufficient detail that information will be understandable weeks, months, or even several years in the future, in case you have a question about a certain expenditure. Record the expiration date or length of subscriptions when you record a check for a newspaper subscription. Include the length of coverage, along with the name of the payee, in check entries for automobile, homeowners, and life insurance premiums. An entry for a check to a department store or discount store should list the item(s) purchased. Using a check register (which you probably will retain for a long time) to record this important information will provide one convenient record for future reference. It is also good practice to record this same information on the checks you write, because it may occasionally be necessary to provide proof that you paid for something.

Use a bonus or windfall to reduce the balance on a loan. Every so often money seems to fall from heaven. Maybe you unexpectedly inherit money from an aunt, win a lottery prize, receive a modest end-of-year bonus, or collect more than expected from an insurance settlement. These bonuses and windfalls offer a perfect opportunity to reduce your debts. Of course, you can always bank the bonus, which isn't a bad idea. But you are probably paying a higher interest rate on loans than you would be earning from additional savings. Paying off an outstanding credit card balance on which you are being charged an annual interest rate of 15 percent is the same as investing money at an after-tax return of 15 percent.

Use direct deposit. Direct deposit speeds funds to your checking, savings, money market, or mutual fund account at the same time it saves the time and effort of making deposits in person. Direct deposit also saves postage if you ordinarily mail deposits to your account. Direct deposit is available for Social Security payments and it may be offered by your employer. Direct deposit is also often available for dividend and interest payments you receive from investments. If you have avoided direct deposits because of concern about payments being made to the wrong account or arriving late, ease your mind in the first several months of direct deposits by calling the financial institution that will be receiving the deposits. Keep in mind that you will receive timely notices of direct deposits from the paying institutions.

Use ATM or debit cards for cash needs when you travel. Obtaining cash from ATM machines when you are traveling is more convenient and often more economical than using traveler checks. The cards are especially convenient when you travel abroad, where financial institutions often charge a fee or offer a poor exchange rate for both cash and traveler checks. A charge of $1 is generally levied for each cash advance on an ATM or debit card regardless of the amount of funds you require. Thus, while you pay an average 1 percent of face value for traveler's checks, you can withdraw from an ATM the equivalent of $500 of a foreign currency for a fee of $1, or two-tenths of one percent of the amount withdrawn. Of course, funds must be available in your account in order for you to take advantage of these cards, because the cash received is immediately subtracted from your account.

When purchasing something from a business, make your check payable to the business, not a person. Why would the person who assists you request that you make out the check to him or her? For one thing, a person running a small business may be able to hide the payment from tax authorities by depositing the check into a personal account instead of the business account. A dishonest employee may intend to cash the check and hide the payment from the business. You will be unable to prove the bill has been paid if you can produce only a canceled check made out to an individual. It is also a good policy to write the item or service purchased in the lower left corner of each check.

Participate in your employer's medical set-aside program (also called a flexible spending account). Many employers offer programs in which a portion of your gross income is set aside in an account that can be used to pay your family's medical expenses. Funds in the account can be used to pay the deductible and co-payment portion of your health insurance. The account can also be used to pay charges that qualify as medical expenses in calculating your federal tax liability that are not covered by your health insurance plan, for example, the cost of eyeglasses. The beauty of the program is that contributions to the account reduce your taxable income. If you instruct your employer to deduct $100 monthly from your paycheck, taxable income for the year will be reduced by 12 times $100, or $1,200. You are required to specify the amount to be deducted each pay-check before the start of each year. Deductions can be changed during the year only for specified events such as marriage, divorce, loss of a spouse or child, or birth of a child. You are not permitted to reduce deductions during the last quarter of the year if you determine in September that you will be unable to spend all the funds in your account. Also, unused funds in the account at year end are forfeited. In other words, be conservative in the amount you instruct your employer to deduct.

Place your IRA with an institution that does not charge a fee. Sufficient competition for IRA funds exists that some institutions, and most commercial banks and savings-and-loan associations, do not charge either a setup fee or an annual maintenance fee. Seek out these institutions and avoid this unnecessary cost, which will have the effect of reducing the funds you have available for retirement. Many brokerage firms charge both fees. Some brokerage companies charge up to $50 to establish an IRA and then charge another $35 to $50 annually to maintain the account. This is in addition to commissions you pay to buy or sell investments. Take advantage of the savings possible by placing your IRA with one of the institutions that do not charge either type fee.

Discuss money before marriage. Love is important, but it's not the only thing that holds a marriage together. Money problems are at the root of many failed marriages. It is best to have some straight talk about important monetary matters before you walk down the aisle. Who will manage your financial assets and income? Will you and your spouse

FACTORS FOR CALCULATING
FUTURE DOLLAR AMOUNTS

Annual Rate of Increase

No. of Years	2%	3%	4%	5%	6%	7%	8%	9%
1	1.020	1.030	1.040	1.050	1.060	1.070	1.080	1.090
2	1.040	1.061	1.082	1.102	1.124	1.145	1.166	1.189
3	1.060	1.093	1.093	1.125	1.191	1.225	1.260	1.295
4	1.082	1.126	1.170	1.216	1.263	1.311	1.361	1.412
5	1.104	1.159	1.217	1.276	1.338	1.403	1.469	1.539
6	1.126	1.194	1.265	1.340	1.418	1.501	1.587	1.677
7	1.149	1.230	1.316	1.407	1.504	1.606	1.714	1.828
8	1.172	1.267	1.369	1.478	1.594	1.718	1.851	1.993
9	1.195	1.305	1.423	1.551	1.690	1.838	1.999	2.172
10	1.219	1.344	1.480	1.629	1.791	1.967	2.159	2.367
15	1.346	1.558	1.801	2.079	2.397	2.759	3.172	3.642
20	1.486	1.806	2.191	2.653	3.207	3.870	4.661	5.604
25	1.641	2.094	2.666	3.386	4.292	5.427	6.848	8.623
30	1.812	2.427	3.243	4.322	5.744	7.612	10.060	13.270

maintain separate checking accounts? Do you each plan to have your own credit cards? Will all your assets be in joint name or do you plan to own assets separately? How much money do each of you currently owe? What happens to the assets that each of you brings into the marriage, especially if one brings in substantially more assets than the other? If you or your spouse-to-be has previously been married, are there any lingering financial commitments? Arguments about money management can "crash" a marriage; it is crucial to bring your financial affairs out in the open prior to the big date so that later misunderstandings are minimized.

Prearrange for your bank or other financial institution to cover checks for which insufficient funds are available. Writing a bad check has always been bad news, and it is fast becoming even worse news as financial institutions increase the fees charged for this occasional indiscretion. You may also discover that an additional fee is charged by the business that took the check. Even the most careful and honest individual can occasionally write a check for which insufficient funds are available. You may use faulty math in calculating your checking account balance, or you may not receive credit for a deposit on the expected date. Protect yourself against being embarrassed, having a black mark in your credit file, and being penalized by the financial institution that holds your checking account by contacting the institution and prearranging for coverage of a bad check. If you maintain a savings account at the institution, arrange for an automatic funds transfer (AFT) from savings to checking to cover any deficiency. You can also sign an agreement for an automatic overdraft loan that will cover a bad check by borrowing funds on your VISA® or MasterCard® account. These loans are sometimes subject to minimums, something you should ask about when you arrange for the coverage.

Keep the balance in your savings and checking accounts below the maximum covered by federal insurance. Although the $100,000 limit for federal insurance sounds like a lot of money (and it is!), the aggregate balances of all your accounts in a single institution may creep above this amount. Several certificates of deposit, a savings account, a money market deposit account, and a checking account that are all at the same bank, credit union, or savings-and-loan association, may result in the aggregate balances exceeding the federal insurance limit. The insurance limit applies to all of the accounts, not each of the accounts, at a single institution. Because financial institutions tend to be very competitive, there is no compelling reason to maintain all your financial assets at one institution anyway. Spread your business around. You will obtain more insurance coverage and at the same time receive more pens, key chains, matches, and paperweights.

Pay by check or credit card if there is any reason to think you may later need proof of payment. You may occasionally be called upon to produce proof that you paid a particular bill. The local newspaper may improperly credit your payment and terminate the subscription early. The local utility may misdirect your payment to someone else's account and subsequently bill you for two months' service. These slipups occasionally occur, and you need to be able to produce evidence that bills have been paid. Although you can always ask for receipts when you pay cash, these are easily misplaced or discarded.

Involve yourself in your family's financial affairs. Marriages are frequently one-sided when it comes to managing the family finances. One person takes care of paying the bills, getting the taxes done, balancing the checkbook, and investing the surplus. It's all too easy to let your spouse take care of all the financial affairs. But what happens if your spouse files for divorce? How do you obtain a fair settlement when you may not even know what you own? If your spouse pre-deceases you, what will happen to your financial affairs? You need to be involved in your family's financial affairs to protect yourself. The time you invest in learning what you own and where it is located is an insurance policy for which you are the beneficiary.

Ask your bank if you will benefit by linking your checking and savings accounts. Some financial institutions allow you to combine the balances in your checking account and savings account for purposes of calculating fees. The institution may charge a monthly fee if your checking account balance falls below a prescribed level. Linking balances in the two accounts may make it easier for you to meet the institution's required minimum and avoid a monthly fee. Linking accounts may also allow you to earn a higher return on your savings account, if the institution pays higher returns on progressively higher balances. In any case, you lose nothing by accepting this option.

Look for an alternative to an expensive checking account. If you maintain a relatively low checking account balance, your financial institution may sock you with a monthly fee of from $5 to $10. The fees keep increasing as financial institutions seek to make each of their services self-supporting. Over a period of years, this relatively small monthly fee adds up to a substantial sum of money. You may be able to do better at another financial institution, especially a credit union. Credit unions offer share draft accounts (analogous to checking accounts) and often charge only a nominal fee, or no fee at all, even if the balance in your account is relatively small. Credit unions often pay a higher return on account balances. You owe it to yourself to check out the competition. Telephone several banks, savings-and-loan associations, and credit unions (membership is required to open an account) and inquire about their checking services. Examine which alternative offers the best deal for you.

Begin saving for retirement at an early age. The earlier you begin planning for retirement, the more likely it is that you will achieve your goal of a comfortable life after employment. Suppose you wish to accumulate a retirement fund of $250,000 by the time you reach an anticipated retirement age of sixty-five. Assuming your savings earn an annual return of 7 percent, the following annual amounts must be saved to accumulate a retirement fund of $250,000:

Age When Saving Commences	Annual Saving Required
25	$ 1,252
30	1,808
35	2,647
40	3,953
45	6,098
50	9,949
55	18,095
60	43,473

Earning a return greater than 7 percent allows you to achieve the same goal with smaller annual amounts than those shown above; an annual return of under 7 percent requires a larger amount saved each year. The key to a successful and manageable savings program is to begin early, while time is available to accumulate a substantial amount of money with relatively modest annual saving.

Roll over a pension distribution if you change employers. Suppose your pension plan has accumulated a substantial amount of assets during the last ten or fifteen years of employment. If you decide to move to a new job with a different employer, you will be required to determine what to do with the pension accumulation at your current employer. If the pension is paid to you, the distribution will be taxable as ordinary income and may be subject to an additional 10 percent penalty (if you are under fifty-nine and a half years of age, or, in the case of early retirement, fifty-five or under). If, on the other hand, you roll over the distribution within sixty days to your new employer's pension plan, or to an IRA, you can defer taxes on the distribution.

If you decide to retire early, think about using your IRA as a lifetime annuity. Withdrawing funds from an IRA prior to age fifty-nine and a half normally requires that you pay ordinary taxes *plus* a 10 percent tax surcharge on the amount withdrawn. You can avoid the 10 percent penalty if you direct the plan's custodian to distribute equal annual installments based on your life expectancy. You collect payments without penalty regardless of your age at the time the distributions begin, although you must still pay ordinary taxes on each distribution.

Make deposits early enough in the day to receive credit for that day. Many financial institutions, including banks, savings and loans, credit unions, and brokerage firms close out each day's business early in the afternoon. Transactions after a certain time are recorded as occurring on the following day. For example, a local bank may record all deposits received up until 2:00 P.M. in that day's business but record deposits after 2:00 P.M. in the next day's business. Under this system a deposit after 2:00 P.M. is treated the same as a deposit made at noon the following day, thus earning one day less of interest. Making certain you receive an extra day's credit by beating the 2:00 P.M. deadline is not particularly important if you are depositing $120 in a savings account earning a 4 percent annual return (1.3 cents per day). On the other hand, earning an extra day's interest is more significant for an $8,000 deposit in an account earning 7 percent ($1.55 per day). Beating the clock also allows that day's deposits to offset checks or other charges that are processed that day. Ask someone at your institution about the time each day's business is closed.

Don't assume that all investments made at a bank or savings and loan are insured. Certificates of deposit, savings accounts, and checking accounts at insured institutions are safe up to the limit of the insurance. These types of accounts have long been insured by agencies of the federal government, and individuals sometimes assume that all the investment products offered by these same institutions are insured. In fact, financial institutions also offer uninsured products, such as mutual funds and annuities. Bonds purchased through a bank can fluctuate in value and may end up in default. Many individuals lost substantial sums of money by investing in debt securities offered by savings-and-loan associations prior to the savings-and-loan financial debacle. Many of these individuals wrongfully assumed their investments were insured. Always ask if a particular financial product is insured. If in doubt, obtain the answer in writing.

If you are dissatisfied with your IRA's performance, transfer your funds to an IRA at another institution. Just because you opened your IRA at a local financial institution doesn't mean your assets have to remain there until distributions begin. Why invest your funds in a five-year CD that pays 6 percent when high-quality corporate bonds with the same maturity are available with returns of $7\frac{1}{2}$ percent? Funds in an IRA can be moved to another institution by either a direct transfer or a rollover. Many transfer options are available. Funds can be transferred from a bank to a brokerage account, from a savings and loan to a bank, or from a brokerage account to an insurance company. A direct transfer is an institution-to-institution movement of funds in which you do not take possession. This is the cleanest method for moving assets, but it may be slow. The institution to receive the funds will generally assist you with the transfer. The alternative is a rollover in which you withdraw funds from one IRA and personally move the assets to the new account. You must accomplish the transfer within sixty days of the withdrawal; otherwise, the payout is considered a distribution and becomes taxable. Always determine whether a penalty or fee will be assessed if you choose to transfer IRA assets to another institution.

Choose a financial planner who charges by the hour. Financial planners earn their income in one of two ways; by selling products on which they earn commissions, or by charging for their time. The worst case scenario is a financial planner who profits from both. It is important to obtain unbiased financial advice, something you are more likely to receive if the planner provides advice on which you act to purchase products from others. The pitfall of obtaining advice from someone with products to sell is obvious: the advisor is almost sure to promote those particular products and exclude products from others that may be more appropriate or involve lower fees. You are better off paying for the advice, which makes available more options with a more favorable cost structure, than for the products. If you are in doubt, ask if the financial planner receives commissions from the products he or she recommends. If no consulting charge is involved you can count on the financial planner having a vested interest in selling the recommended products.

Have large sums of money wired rather than mailed. Time is money, especially when funds due to you are sent by check in the mail. Suppose you sell $20,000 worth of shares in a mutual fund and wait four days for the check to arrive. The delay means you wait four days to reinvest the funds, thereby losing investment income of approximately $2.00 daily, or a total of $8.00 for four days. The $2.00 of daily lost income assumes the funds could be invested at an annual after-tax return of 3.5 percent. A larger amount of money, a higher return, or a longer delay results in even greater amounts of lost income. Money you are due to receive can be put to use almost immediately if you request that the funds be wired rather than mailed. Wiring funds entails a fee of $10 to $15, but it will be worth the expense if the amount of money is sufficiently large. You usually have to prearrange to wire funds (there is no charge for this), so be certain to complete the necessary paperwork ahead of time. Also inquire about any fee that will be charged.

Establish financial goals. Like most individuals, you probably have certain goals, some clearly defined and others fuzzier. Perhaps you intend to pay most of your children's future college expenses, or you want to retire at 55 years of age. A long and expensive vacation may be in the back of your mind, or something less grand, such as acquiring a new vehicle in four years. Setting forth your financial goals will allow you to determine which goals are most important and which goals are most likely to be achievable. As you identify and rank financial goals, you can estimate the funds you must set aside each month or each year in order to achieve each goal. If you fail to establish and rank financial goals, most of them will remain elusive, and eventually, unachievable.

Fund your retirement plan early in the year. The earlier in the year a retirement plan is funded, the more time each contribution has to accumulate tax-deferred income. Over several decades, early contributions will have a substantial impact on the amount of funds you have available at retirement. Suppose you deposit $2,000 annually for 30 years into an individual retirement account. If the funds in your account earn an 8 percent annual return, the IRA will total $248,176 at the end of thirty years if deposits occur at the beginning of January each year, but only $226,560 if deposits are made at the end of each year. The amount of your retirement fund will be substantially larger when retirement contributions occur early.

Negotiate fees with your bank. Commercial banks, savings-and-loan associations, and credit unions have recently raised fees for many of the services they provide, including issuing cashier's checks, certifying checks, and processing bounced checks. While each financial institution has its own fee schedule for each of these services, you may discover that the fees will be reduced or waived if you request it. Financial institutions want to keep you happy, especially if you are a good customer. If you regularly overdraw your checking account and keep relatively small balances, you have little leverage. On the other hand, if you have a checking account, mortgage, and certificates of deposit with the same institution, you may be able to have the fee for a cashier's check waived. There is nothing to lose and everything to gain buy asking for a fee waiver.

Sign up for a financial institution senior club. Many commercial banks and savings-and-loan associations offer a package of services at a special price to customers who are seniors. For example, participants may receive free checks, no-fee cashier's checks, a reduced lock-box fee, free travelers' checks, and a checking account with no minimum balance requirement—institutions vary in what features they offer. Seniors are often fiscally conservative with sizeable funds, which makes them ideal customers. The special packages are often available at low or even no cost, so you rarely have anything to lose by signing up. If your current institution doesn't offer this type program, scan the local newspapers or call competing institutions to find the deal worthy of moving your account. Of course, you must meet an age requirement, but at many institutions an age of only fifty-five is sufficient to qualify.

Meet the minimum balance requirement in your checking account to avoid a monthly fee. Financial institutions often impose a monthly fee when your checking account balance falls below a prescribed level. For example, a commercial bank may charge $7 in any month the balance in an account falls below $500. Fees and minimums vary by institution, but you are best served by maintaining the minimum, even if funds must be transferred from savings. The key is to view the minimum balance as an investment that earns a return equal to the fee that is avoided. In the example above, $500 maintained in the account would result in annual savings of $7 times 12 months, or $84. The annual return of $84/$500, or 16.8 percent, is much higher than the return the $500 would earn in a savings account. Also consider that the return is nontaxable, because the monthly fee would not be tax deductible. In other words, $84 that is saved each year is on an after-tax basis. The return earned for maintaining a minimum checking balance is reduced when a higher balance is required and/or a lower monthly fee is imposed.

Ask your financial institution how interest is computed on savings. Several methods are utilized by financial institutions to calculate interest paid on savings. Some institutions pay interest only on the lowest balance in an account during the period on which interest is paid. Suppose a bank pays interest quarterly. If $2,000 is in your account from January 1 through February 10, when you deposit an additional $3,000, interest will be paid only on $2,000 for the entire three months. Is this a rip-off, or what? Other institutions pay interest based on first-in, first-out. That is, any withdrawals during the period are assumed to come from the earliest deposits. This also works to your disadvantage and the financial institution's advantage. Another method uses last-in, first-out, in which interest is calculated by assuming withdrawals are made from the most recent deposits. Last and best is the day-of-deposit to day-of-withdrawal method in which interest is paid each day money remains on deposit in your account. If your account has little activity, the method of computing interest will have little impact on your earnings. If you make frequent deposits and withdrawals, however, be sure to inquire about the institution's method of computing interest.

Don't allow your money to remain idle. Money that remains idle doesn't produce income to save or spend. Allowing money to remain idle in your checking account or delaying the deposit of a check reduces your investment income without any advantage to you. This doesn't mean you should drive five miles to the bank to deposit a $2.95 refund check. It does mean you should not permit a "meaningful" amount of money to simply lie around. Put your money to work as soon as possible and increase your investment income. Deposit checks and move checking account balances to more profitable investments sooner rather than later. If you are unsure where you wish to invest your funds, use a money market account or a money market mutual fund as a temporary place to park your funds.

Delay payments from your retirement fund. Just because you retire doesn't mean you have to withdraw money from your IRA or other retirement funds. You will generally benefit financially by first using nonsheltered funds—for example, money from a savings account or certificate of deposit—and only drawing on tax-sheltered funds when non-sheltered funds are exhausted. Leaving sheltered funds alone as long as possible allows these funds to grow without being subject to taxation. Drawing on sheltered funds first causes you to pay taxes on the withdrawals at the same time you are required to pay taxes on income earned by nonsheltered funds. Keep in mind that you are required to begin withdrawing funds from most retirement plans by the age of seventy and a half years.

CHAPTER 7

Shopping
Money Smarts

Keeping current on the local shopping scene by reading the newspaper and browsing through stores can result in substantial savings. Saving vendor coupons until items go on sale will result in double savings. Plan meals around sale items. Always ask for a raincheck when a store is out of an advertised special. Inquire if you qualify for a senior discount. Be patient and wait for good deals to come along.

Plan menus from advertised specials. Many families plan menus on the basis of what sounds good rather than what is on sale. Get the most value for your money by doing just the opposite; plan your menus from sale items. Check the grocery advertisements in your daily newspaper, which usually appear on Wednesday or Thursday, and jot down the sale items. Grocery stores rotate sale items, so you can achieve both variety and reduced prices. For example, certain cuts of beef may be on sale one week, chickens the next. Planning menus around featured sale items will produce substantial savings on your grocery bills.

Buy ahead. Always try to buy ahead so that enough of an item will be available until the next good deal. Don't allow yourself to run out of things, especially durable items that can be stored for relatively long periods. Make a point of stocking backup toilet tissue, spices, coffee, aluminum foil, vitamins, facial tissues, pest spray, canned goods, and so forth, so that you won't have to make extra shopping trips or pay too high a price.

Take full advantage of a good sale. Buy substantial amounts of nonperishable items when the price is right. When a grocery store offers an unusually good price for your favorite brand of coffee, buy in quantity and stockpile as much as your storage space permits. Don't be embarrassed to buy a case of canned fruit when the price is right. If the retailer hasn't established a limit on the number of units that can be purchased, buy all that you think you will use.

Subscribe to the local newspaper. A local newspaper is an excellent source for useful consumer information. Unlike television, magazines, and radio advertising, which mostly pitch useless puffery, newspaper advertisements provide solid information about product availability, rebates, and comparative prices in your area. The classified advertisements alone may be sufficient reason to subscribe, especially if you don't mind owning another person's throwaways. An annual subscription to your local newspaper is one of your best investments. When you subscribe to the paper, remember to ask if any specials are being offered to new subscribers. Newspapers frequently offer specials to build circulation, but you may not receive one if you fail to mention it.

Make a list of the things you need to purchase before you go shopping. Retailers want to convince you to buy the goods and services they sell, regardless of whether you need them! Prepare a list of the businesses you need to visit and the things you need to buy *before* you leave on a shopping trip, when you have time to also think about how much you should pay. At home you can browse the newspaper and use the telephone Yellow Pages to comparison shop. Don't visit a store unprepared and place yourself at the mercy of marketing professionals who judge their success by how much they can entice you to buy. Do your best to stick to the items that are on your list.

Don't buy on impulse. How many people have you seen pick up a box from an aisle display in a grocery store or pull a shirt off the display rack near the entrance to a clothing store. Retailers know that many shoppers are inclined to buy whatever catches their eye, even if they don't need it. If things don't sell, store managers rearrange their displays to encourage impulse buyers to snap up slow-moving merchandise. You are much more likely to buy items you don't need when you shop on impulse, and you will usually pay too much in the process.

Don't assume a product with a brand name is superior to a no-name competitive product. Manufacturers of brand-name merchandise spend huge sums to call your attention to their products. They pay to advertise in the media, sponsor blimps and auto races, and have the rich and famous promote their products. These manufacturers attempt to recover their advertising expenditures by selling more units *at a higher price*. You have probably read about the outrageous prices television networks squeeze from firms that advertise during the Super Bowl, the Olympics, the Academy Awards, and so forth. Who do you think pays for all this advertising? The answer is the individuals who purchase the advertised products. Don't do it! Let someone else pay for multimillion-dollar endorsements.

Buy when prices are lowest. Make an effort to purchase goods and services when prices are typically at their lowest. Buy automobiles during a dreary winter day when shoppers are scarce, dealers are desperate, and car lots are bulging with inventory. Buy winter clothes in the spring, and summer clothes in the fall. Buy vegetables when they are abundant and cheap, and buy firewood out of season. Make long-distance calls on the weekends and go to the movie theater during the matinee special. Buy when others aren't, and you are likely to get a better deal.

Don't be ashamed to ask for a discount if you are a senior. Many businesses offer discounts to senior citizens, and the number will only increase as a greater proportion of citizens reach the "golden years." Restaurants, motels, movie theaters, theme parks, and pharmacies are just a few of the establishments that regularly provide seniors with discounts of 10 percent or more. Some fast food establishments provide discounts or a free or reduced-cost beverage. Some grocery stores give modest senior discounts on a certain day of the week. While you may not save a bundle, small amounts add up to significant savings over time. Obtaining a discount certainly doesn't require much effort on your part; just ask. Be aware that many establishments allow you to qualify for senior discounts at an age of less than sixty-five. Being over sixty, or even fifty-five, may qualify you for a senior discount. Don't be bashful about asking for a senior discount, ask why the discount isn't bigger.

Request a rain check when a store is out of an advertised special. Most retailers attempt to have adequate stocks of advertised specials. Managers know that customers become upset when they are unable to buy an advertised product, especially after making a special trip to the store. Unfortunately, stores have limited storage space, and particularly good deals may generate so much business that stock is temporarily depleted. Don't look at the empty shelf, mumble to yourself, and move to the next item on your list. Ask the customer service department for a rain check, and do it before you forget and leave the store. Make sure that the rain check allows you to purchase as many units as you want, or as many as the advertisement indicated. You can always buy less than the quantity indicated on the rain check.

Don't look for things to buy. Do you stroll the malls and browse the stores, searching for things to purchase, even though you can't think of anything in particular you need? Do you return home with new clothing and kitchen appliances, even though your closets are full and you rarely cook? When shopping becomes a major leisure activity, you can count on overspending. Don't use spare time to search for things to buy; you will end up spending money you can't afford for things that should have remained in the store.

Don't always be the first to buy the latest item. If you tend to be among the first to try a new product or service, you are often paying too high a price. This isn't always true, of course, because some manufacturers offer special prices or coupons to entice consumers to try new products. Still, new products and services are often scarce because many people want to be first at everything. Popular new models of automobiles are frequently in short supply and priced at top dollar. Likewise, popular movies play at full price to full houses, even though you can wait six months and save half or more when the movie begins running in smaller theaters. Wait another six months and you will be able to rent the video so that the whole family can view the movie for $2 to $3. Fashions work the same way. The newest nearly always brings the highest price. Wait a while and buy the same thing at a clearance sale.

Use the telephone for local shopping. It's a lot cheaper to price shop using your telephone than to drive all over town looking for the lowest price. Do you need a piece of hardware? Call several discount stores or hardware stores and compare the prices. Depending on the item you need, one or more stores are likely to be out of stock anyway. Vehicles are costly to operate, and comparison shopping in person is expensive. On the other hand, local telephone calls don't cost anything. Be forewarned that many grocery stores don't list their telephone numbers, partly because they don't want consumers such as yourself calling about prices.

Consider energy efficiency when you buy an appliance. Energy efficiency should be an important consideration when you purchase a long-lived appliance. Energy-efficient appliances nearly always carry a higher price tag, partly because they cost more to manufacture. Energy savings, however, can more than offset the higher initial cost of an appliance, often fairly rapidly. For example, refrigerators typically last for many years and result in cumulative electric bills that amount to much more than the initial cost. Substantial overall savings can be achieved if you purchase an energy-efficient model that saves 30 to 40 percent of the electricity used by an ordinary model. The bottom line is that energy consumption, as well as the initial price, matters in choosing an appliance. The lowest price can sometimes result in the highest long-term cost.

Shop for the lowest prescription drug prices. Prescription drug prices can vary substantially from one pharmacy to the next. Always price shop before ordering a prescription, because you will probably return to the same pharmacy when it is time for a refill. Keep in mind that many pharmacies will match or better the prices of competitors. Even if you prefer to do business at a particular pharmacy (convenient location, free delivery, or a likable pharmacist), shop around and inform your pharmacist of competitors' lower prices. Nearly all pharmacies have listed phone numbers, so comparison shop by telephone. Prescriptions can be transferred to a different pharmacy if your current pharmacy becomes uncompetitive.

Be observant when you check out at a store. Always make it a point to observe the amounts that are being rung up on the register when you check out of a store. Even modern scanners produce occasional mistakes, generally in the store's favor. Mistakes don't occur because the store is attempting to cheat its customers. Rather, they result from 1) the checker entering the wrong price, 2) an incorrect shelf price, 3) an incorrect price tag on the item being purchased, or 4) an incorrect price programmed into the scanning system. The most common mistake is being charged full price for a sale item. If you are unloading the cart while the checker processes your order, you won't be able to observe the register. Ask the checker to begin only after you complete the unloading. An alternative is to examine the register tape after the order is processed, but this works only if you purchase a few items; it takes too long if you have several bags of items, and if you wait until you arrive home you may not have the energy to return to the store to correct a minor overring. Take care of business at the business.

Ask the salesperson if something you are about to purchase will soon be on sale. Everyone has bought something only to find the same item on sale several days later. Discouraging, isn't it? Buying just prior to a sale is most common with groceries and clothing simply because these items are purchased frequently, but the same misstep can occur when you purchase appliances, automobiles, and most other products. One way to help avoid this frustration is to ask the salesperson if the price will be reduced in the near future. Most salespeople are honest and will inform you of upcoming sales, allowing you to delay the purchase for substantial savings. Even when no sale is scheduled, asking the question sometimes prompts the salesperson to dicker on price. It puts the salesperson on notice that you are sensitive to the price and they may lose the sale unless you are offered a better deal.

Purchase Christmas and birthday gifts throughout the year. You are most likely to pay too much for unappreciated gifts when you buy in a hurry. Wait until a few days before Christmas and you will probably be willing to purchase nearly anything at whatever price the store posts. The key to obtaining the best gifts at bargain prices is to shop throughout the year. Keep your eyes open for appropriate gifts for upcoming birthdays, weddings, births, Christmas, and so forth. If you discover a good deal on a particular item, buy several units that can be stored until appropriate occasions arise. Use after-Christmas sales to purchase presents for the following Christmas.

Share the costs with others when ordering from a catalog that requires a minimum handling and postage fee. Remember thumbing through a catalog and discovering the perfect blouse or pair of shoes, only to find that the shipping charge was nearly half the cost of the item you were interested in buying? Catalog orders often require a minimum handling and/or postage fee that makes it expensive to place small orders. Some catalog companies reduce or waive handling fees on orders of a minimum size. Other firms offer reduced prices when minimum quantities are ordered. Lower prices or reduced handling and postage charges can also be achieved by finding other individuals who are interested in ordering from the same catalog. Perhaps your friends, co-workers, or members of the bridge club would be interested in placing an order. Circulate the catalog among prospective buyers before placing an order. After all, if you like what you see and the prices are right, your friends may appreciate the chance to place an order too.

Establish a Christmas budget. Christmas bills (not bells) can cause financial headaches that last through the fourth of July. It is good financial management to establish a budget for the Christmas gifts you plan to buy for friends and family members. Determine the total amount you can spend for Christmas without straining your budget, then allocate that sum among the gifts you expect to purchase. Remember, everyone doesn't need to receive gifts of equal value. Establishing an overall budget for Christmas will force you to reconsider expensive presents that cause reduced spending for presents to others.

Stockpile cents-off coupons until products go on sale. You can achieve substantially more bang for the buck by holding cents-off coupons until the appropriate products are offered at sale prices. Manufacturers frequently distribute cents-off coupons and later offer special deals to retailers that temporarily reduce the prices of these items. Increase your savings by waiting to use coupons on sale-priced merchandise. Temporarily file away vendor coupons from the Sunday newspaper to see if the manufacturer or a local retailer offers the product at a special price. The remember to

TYPICAL EXPENDITURE PATTERNS
BY INCOME CLASSIFICATION, 1992

Item	Annual Income Before Taxes		
	$5,000 to $9,999	$20,000 to $29,999	$50,000 to $69,999
Food at home	$ 1,666	$ 2,558	$ 3,562
Food away from home	509	1,406	2,712
Tobacco and alcohol	319	621	815
Shelter	2,661	4,576	7,941
Household operations and supplies	413	715	1,411
Utilities, fuels, and pub. services	1,349	1,859	2,559
Household furnishings	357	1,020	1,856
Apparel	636	1,564	2,780
Private transportation	1,555	4,672	7,675
Public transportation	97	233	439
Health care	1,046	1,648	2,087
Personal care products	181	377	604
Entertainment	436	1,159	2,679
Education/reading	277	325	878
Miscellaneous	283	637	1,224
Cash contributions	191	688	1,421
Personal insurance/pensions	284	2,013	6,152
Total annual expenditures	$12,260	$26,071	$46,795

Source: Bureau of Labor Statistics, U.S. Department of Labor, *Consumer Expenditures in 1992*

use the coupons before they expire. Coupons without expiration dates are particularly valuable because you can wait months or even years for a good sale.

Buy extra copies of newspapers that contain particularly valuable coupons. Many Sunday newspapers are packed with valuable coupons. Newspapers also sometimes contain rebate forms that allow you to recover a portion or all of an item's cost. If a newspaper contains several valuable coupons and rebate offers, it may be worthwhile to purchase extra copies. A Sunday newspaper coupon section that contains a dozen or so coupons that will save $4 or $5 certainly pays back the extra $1.50 per copy to purchase extra copies. Although retailers typically establish a limit of one coupon per item purchased, multiple coupons can be used by purchasing multiple units of the product.

Substitute a generic for a brand name drug. U.S. pharmaceutical companies that develop a new drug are granted an exclusive right to produce that drug for 17 years. After the patent expires at the end of seventeen years, other pharmaceutical companies are permitted to produce and sell the chemical equivalent of the drug with the approval of the Food and Drug Administration. The chemical equivalent, or generic version, is often considerably less expensive than the brand name drug. When your physician prescribes a drug, ask if a generic equivalent is available, and, if so, whether the generic version can be substituted. If you forget to ask the physician, ask the pharmacist who fills the prescription. Substituting a generic version of a brand name can save money both for you and your insurance company.

Don't spend $1.00 for gasoline in order to save 25 cents on a loaf of bread. It often doesn't make economic sense to drive all over town to save a little here and a little there. Small amounts add up, of course, but maybe not to enough to offset the transportation expense of achieving the savings. You should also consider the time consumed in your shopping odyssey. When thinking about driving to a store to purchase several sale items, calculate the savings you expect and compare it to the expense of making the trip (use 20 cents per mile). If it is a close call, the economics of the trip probably don't make sense.

Consider what you will be required to give up if you make a purchase. Choosing to buy something means you are surrendering money that could be used to purchase something else. Economists call whatever you must give up the *opportunity cost* of the purchase you make. Even the time spent on an activity entails an opportunity cost. The opportunity cost of watching an Atlanta Braves baseball game is mowing the yard, going to the grocery store, or studying for a test. Buy a new car and you give up several vacations, a year of college for your child, or six months of early retirement. Eat at a restaurant and you give up a movie. Buying something entails an opportunity cost regardless of whether you pay cash or borrow. In fact, borrowing money required for a purchase will result in interest charges and create an additional cost.

If a store establishes a limit on an advertised sale item, go through the checkout more than once. A store-imposed limit on the unit number of a sale item a customer is permitted to purchase is a great scourge to the conscientious shopper. A discount store or grocery store may advertise four cans of tomatoes for $1.00, but impose a limit of four cans per customer. Additional purchases must be made at the regular price of 49 cents per can. Once you've incurred the trouble and expense of visiting the store, you might as well make it worth your while by loading up on advertised items. Rather than being limited to buying only four cans, go through the checkout three different times and buy twelve cans. If you feel uncomfortable with repeat purchases at the same checkout, use different checkout lines so you won't be recognized by the checkers. The truth is, most checkers couldn't care less. As an alternative, have other members of your family accompany you to the store so that each member can purchase up to the allowed limit.

Buy health and beauty aids at a discount store, not a grocery store. Toothpaste, shampoo, soap, aspirin, and other health and beauty aids are convenient to purchase during one of your frequent shopping trips to the grocery store, but these items usually cost less at discount department stores. Grocery stores are a good place to buy groceries, but not most other items unless the grocery store has a particularly good sale. Even then, you may be able to locate the same item at a lower price at a discount store. When was the last time you found a good deal on dental floss at a grocery store?

Shop at stores that double or triple the face value of your coupons, but limit your purchases to items for which you have coupons. Stores that double and triple coupon values (for example, value a 25-cent coupon at 50 cents or 75 cents), usually offer reduced costs only on those items for which you have coupons. Stores that double and triple coupon values normally compensate for the bonus on vendor coupons by charging higher prices than competitors who offer everyday low prices. Take advantage of the coupon bonus without buying other items for which you don't have coupons. Also avoid buying high-priced items on which you have relatively small coupons. Make it a policy in these stores to match the number of coupons you use with the number of items you purchase.

Use the last-in, first-out method when you purchase groceries. Grocery stores sell the oldest goods first (first-in, first-out) by moving older goods to the front of the shelf and placing the newest, freshest items at the back of the shelf. Shoppers solve the manager's problem of getting rid of old merchandise by selecting the most readily available units (those at the front of the shelf). Why purchase a store's oldest goods when you can just as easily buy the newest items at the same price? Reach for items at the back, not the front of the shelf. Freshness is particularly important when you buy perishable items such as fruits and vegetables, dairy goods, breads and other bakery items, and snacks. Dated items such as packaged dairy goods can have expiration dates a month or more apart. Likewise, it is not uncommon to find milk cartons side by side, with expiration dates up to a week apart. Fortunately, most dairy goods have the expiration dates printed somewhere on the container. When items do not include an expiration date (or have a coded date), assume that the freshest units will be the most difficult to reach.

Examine the marked prices on goods you are planning to purchase. Stores that price and tag individual units of the same item (rather than scan UPC codes) often include different units of the same item marked with different prices. For example, bottles of a particular brand of car wax may be marked at $3.59 at the same time that identical bottles of the wax are marked at $2.99. Some stores don't change the prices on already-marked merchandise when new goods are stocked at a different price. Store employees sometimes accidentally mark merchandise with an incorrect price. You are not cheating the store to choose the item with the lower price tag since there isn't any way to know which price is correct. What you do know is that the lower price is the right price for you. As surprising as it may seem, it really isn't unusual to find different units of the same item marked with different prices.

Pay by credit card when you buy by mail. Paying for mail order items with a credit card provides advantages that paying by check does not. First, depending on the purchase date and billing cycle of your statement, you won't have to come up with the money for twenty-five to fifty-five days following the purchase date. More important, recourse is available in the event you aren't satisfied with the merchandise purchased with a credit card. You can notify the credit card company and contest the payment if merchandise hasn't been delivered or is unsatisfactory. The credit card company will withhold payment to the seller until the dispute is resolved. You are in a much weaker position if you have paid by check. The seller may agree to refund your money or ship a replacement, but what recourse is available if your complaint goes unanswered? The seller already has your money, and although you probably have legal recourse, it is often difficult and expensive to pursue it.

Determine handling and postage charges before you order from a catalog. Catalogs often seem to offer good prices, until you take into account the postage and handling charges that will be added. Often, a minimum fee of $3 to $5 makes a small order uneconomical, even if no sales tax will be charged. Be certain to investigate charges for shipping and handling before you place an order. Add these charges to the price you will be paying to determine if you are really getting a good deal.

Get together friends or co-workers and buy in bulk. You can generally, but not always, save by buying in quantity. The problem is that you may not be able to utilize the amount of goods required to obtain a lower price. Talk to relatives, friends, and co-workers to see whether they might be interested in a good deal. For example, you may want to ask your produce store about the cost of a case of navel oranges and compare the per-orange price with that of oranges purchased individually. If the case price is low enough, you can probably find several other individuals willing to take a quarter case. Arrange the same deal for apples, tomatoes, or even kiwi fruit. Anything that is difficult to store or consume alone is fair game.

Calculate the unit cost before making a purchase. Manufacturers and retailers continually attempt to pull the wool over consumers' eyes. They may reduce the volume or weight of a package slightly without changing the price. For example, while you are accustomed to seeing fruits and vegetables in

16-ounce cans, some firms include only 15 ounces of content *even though the can appears to be the same size.* Is this tricky, or what? You may find only 28 ounces of sauce in a jar, when most competitors use 32-ounce jars. Look for the same trick from soft drink companies, peanut butter manufacturers, snack firms, and so on. Always check the volume of a can, box, or package when you are shopping. What appears to be the least expensive choice may not be. If a store utilizes unit pricing, the price per unit or per ounce will be posted. If need be, take along a small calculator when you go shopping so that you can calculate the cost per unit.

Save receipts so you can obtain a refund if the price is reduced. Many stores will refund the difference between the price you paid and the sale price, if you have purchased an item within a certain period, say thirty days. The policy varies by retailer, but a receipt will certainly be required to obtain the refund. Call the store to determine its policy. If the store does not refund the difference on a recently reduced sale item, don't lose hope. Return the item you purchased for a refund, then buy the same item at the sale price. Many smart shoppers do this. Again, you need the receipt from the original purchase to prove you paid regular price, not the sale price. If you used the item so that it cannot be returned for a refund, buy an additional item at the sale price and return that item using the receipt from your purchase at the regular price.

If you join a book club, record club, or CD club, get out as soon as the commitment is fulfilled. Many club memberships offer good deals. For example, one music club offers from eight to ten CDs or cassette tapes for the price of one.

You are able to acquire a good assortment of CDs or tapes for an average price of $3.00 to $4.00, including shipping, handling, and postage. Likewise, one paperback book club advertises an introductory offer of three books for $1.00 each. Even with postage and handling this is a great bargain. Are these companies just being good Samaritans? Not really. The idea is to hook you with a good deal, then keep you as a member purchasing tapes, CDs, or books at regular price. Beat this system by discontinuing the membership as soon as your commitment is met. Send a letter canceling your membership after you have received your free CDs and purchased the one required CD. Likewise, drop the book club membership at the same time you send payment for the introductory shipment. If you want more CDs or books, have your spouse or a friend join so that you can enjoy another introductory offer.

Try to return merchandise for cash rather than a store credit. When returning a recently purchased item, you are likely to be offered a store credit to be used for subsequent purchases. Always ask for a cash refund in place of a store credit. Some stores have a policy of only giving credits for returned merchandise. Other stores will give cash or credit, but try to talk customers into accepting credit. Accepting a store credit permits the store to keep your money, while you are limited to making a future purchase at that same store. It is to your advantage to get cash. After all, you paid with cash in the first place.

Be flexible in what you will accept. Better deals are available to those who remain flexible about the products and services they will accept. The more narrowly you define the product you want, the more likely you are to pay top dollar for it. Suppose you want to purchase a new automobile. If you demand a specific brand, model, color, and options, few dealers will be able to meet your requirements, leaving you with less bargaining power. You will be unable to play one dealer against another. On the other hand, if several colors or combinations of options are acceptable, you'll stand a much better chance of obtaining a favorable price because you'll have more places to shop. You'll save even more on simple purchases such as paper towels if you are flexible regarding brand. Demanding some particular brand or color of paper towel may make it impossible to purchase towels on sale. The same rule applies to paint, pest spray, toilet paper, clothes, and nearly every other item you may find reason to purchase.

Don't buy anything unless you first know the price. Tricky retailers sometimes fail to post prices in hopes that you will buy without knowing the cost. Have you seen a restaurant menu that doesn't include prices? Keep walking, because you can count on paying too much. How about a candy counter that doesn't display prices? Expect to pay too much if you purchase some. Gasoline stations that fail to post prices of the various grades do so for a reason—their prices aren't competitive with prices being charged at neighboring stations. Have you walked into a tavern or restaurant and ordered a beer or glass of wine without asking the price? You were probably surprised when the bill came. Don't buy anything unless you first know how much you will be required to pay. Good deals, even reasonable deals, have posted prices. Overpriced goods and services are often offered without posted prices. Don't be a sucker.

Buy bargain-priced used books to trade at second-hand bookstores. Used bookstores generally offer paperbacks at half the published price and give you one-quarter the listed price in trade for your books. This allows you to trade two books of your own for one book with an equal list price. Trading puts to good use the used books of little market value that you are unlikely to read again. Another key to cheap reading is to purchase books at garage sales, flea markets, thrift stores, and public libraries, which often sell used paperbacks for 25 cents to 50 cents. When you locate one of these sales, purchase the books that have the highest list prices (assuming the books all sell at the same low price); they will have the greatest value in trade at a used bookstore. A paperback with a $5.95 list price will have a trade value of approximately $1.50, a real bargain even if you have no interest in reading that particular book. Buy ten of these relatively high-priced paperbacks for between $2.50 and $5.00 and you will have trading material to receive $15 in credits toward half-priced books.

Organize vendor coupons. Most shoppers leave large numbers of coupons unused because they can't locate them when needed. Remember the last time you purchased shredded cheese and were unable to come up with the 40-cent coupon you had recently clipped from the Sunday newspaper? If you take time to clip coupons, you should devote time to organize them. With relatively few coupons at any one time, you may be able to get by with a business envelope for storage. A larger number of coupons may require an expanding "check organizer" with pockets that allow you to categorize the coupons. Choose categories such as canned goods, frozen goods, dairy goods, drinks, cereals, and so forth. Select categories that best suit your shopping pattern. Periodically examine the coupons in order to identify those with nearby expiration dates. Don't clutter the envelope with coupons you probably won't use. Why save coupons for sugar-coated cereals when you always eat Cheerios?

Don't delay in making a shopping list of sale items. It is best to make a shopping list during your first reading of a newspaper. Filing the paper away with the intention of making a list later will result in no list at all. Also, the sooner you make the list, the more likely that you will stop at the stores where you need to shop without having to make a special last-minute trip. Delay can cost you money.

Shop for groceries on a full stomach. This old tip is worth repeating. Great willpower is required to pass the clever displays in a grocery store without picking up something, especially if the store has an in-house deli and bakery. Grocery retailers are pros at getting customers to purchase things they don't intend to buy when they walked in the front door. The best way to avoid these purchases is to fill your tummy with food before shopping for groceries. If you're stuffed to the gills before you go grocery shopping, you'll be less tempted to pick up ice cream, candy bars, sweet rolls, potato salad, or sandwich meat. Food, even a Snickers bar, doesn't look nearly as delicious on a full stomach. Nearly everything on the shelves looks good to a hungry shopper.

Buy conservative clothing. The more conservative the clothing, the longer the clothes will remain in style, and the more use you will get out of them. Most clothes don't wear out (unless you are a young child), they just go out of style and hang in the far end of your closet. If you don't believe this, browse through the clothing section of your local Goodwill Store or Salvation Army Thrift Shop. These stores contain racks of functional, but dated, clothing. It is to your advantage to choose clothes with a long fashion life that can be worn for long periods. Oxford cloth shirts with button-down collars will still be in style when the Chicago Cubs win the World Series.

Ask for a cash discount. Stores may offer customers a cash discount, but only when asked. The next time you are at the checkout with merchandise to purchase, ask the cashier if you will receive a discount for paying cash. If you are turned down, pull out a credit card for use as payment. Retailers must pay credit card companies a fee of up to 5 percent of the transaction. Thus, retailers receive only $95 to $97 for a $100 sale charged on a credit card. The fee a retailer pays depends on a variety of factors, including the volume of its credit card business. If the retailer benefits when you pay cash, why shouldn't you receive a portion of the saving? Some retailers also accept less for cash because, although it is illegal, they can pocket a cash payment rather than report it as income, thus saving taxes. You are more likely to receive a discount for cash in a small- to intermediate-size independent store operated by the owner. You will be wasting your breath in large grocery stores, fast-food establishments, and stores that are part of large national chains.

Buy the cheaper cuts of meat, pieces of poultry, and types of fish. The next time you shop for meat, poultry, or fish at the supermarket, save money by scaling down to less expensive, but not necessarily less tasty, choices. Sirloin steak not only costs less per pound than ribeye steak, it has substantially less fat, which means it is a healthier choice. Even better is a piece of chuck roast (if the price is right). Select chicken leg quarters and save two-thirds or more compared to the price charged for breasts. Buy small or medium rather than large shrimp and save several dollars per pound with no loss of quality. Comparable savings are often available on fish as well. Skip the varieties that are in short supply and therefore sell at a premium price. Don't have your mind made up regarding a choice of meat before you enter the store. Compare the prices of various cuts and select the best buy.

Avoid buying at convenience stores. Convenience stores are monuments to consumers who buy things without regard to price. With few exceptions, such as milk, gasoline, and cigarettes, most items offered by convenience stores sell at comparatively high prices. Most convenience store purchases are the result of poor planning; you run out of bathroom tissue or aspirin when it is not possible or inconvenient to get to the supermarket or discount store. Or you forgot something at the supermarket. The latter problem could be solved by taking time to make a shopping list before visiting the supermarket or discount store. Convenience store stops should always be a last resort.

CHAPTER 8

Tax Money Smarts

L earn to calculate your own federal and state income taxes so you gain the knowledge to achieve significant tax savings. You may benefit from bunching itemized deductions every other year and using the standard deduction in alternate years. Consider state taxes when you decide on a place to live. Don't make investment decisions based solely on avoidance of taxes.

Consider bunching your tax deductions. When calculating annual federal income taxes you can choose between the standard deduction and itemized deductions. The full amount of the standard deduction can be used regardless of the actual deductions to which you are entitled. Bunching itemized deductions in alternate years allows you to maximize the use of these deductions and reduce your tax liability. In other years when few deductions are available you will be able to claim the standard deduction. For example, make next year's planned charitable contributions one year early and combine the deductions with this year's contributions. You may be able to bunch certain state and local tax payments in alternate years as well. Itemize in the year when you have lots of deductions and use the standard deduction the following year. During the year you use the standard deduction, delay deductible expenses until the following year.

Move to a state that doesn't tax personal income. You may find that state income taxes eat away an ever larger portion of your income. States have resorted to legalized gambling, increased fees, and *higher taxes* as they struggle to generate additional revenues. Despite the grab for your pocketbook several states, including Florida, Nevada, New Hampshire, Texas, and Washington, still do not levy a personal income tax. Moving from a state that levies a relatively high income tax (*e.g.,* California and New York) to a state with no income tax can substantially increase your disposable income. Current employment may make it difficult to move now or in the near future, but keep the possibility in mind for retirement.

Make charitable gifts with appreciated property that has been held for over a year. Under the current tax law you are permitted to donate appreciated property to a charitable organization and escape taxation on the gain in value. Suppose you purchased one hundred shares of General Motors common stock for $4,000 several years ago, and the stock has a current value of $5,800. If you sell the stock and donate the money, you will pay income taxes on the $1,800 realized gain. On the other hand, donate the stock to a charitable organization and you will gain a deduction for the full $5,800 *and not pay any taxes on the $1,800 gain.* Of course $5,800 is a lot of money and may be more than you typically contribute to a single charity. If so, limit contributions to 10 or 20 shares and still benefit from being able to deduct the full value of the contributions without being required to pay taxes on the gain in value of the shares you give away.

Don't allow too much to be withheld from your paycheck. Some of your friends may brag about the large tax refund they recently received from the state or the U.S. Treasury. A tax refund sounds good but actually represents poor financial planning because it results from having paid too much in taxes. Receiving a refund means your friends have provided the government with an interest-free loan. Tax refunds nearly always result from being overwithheld by an employer. The amount of taxes withheld from your paycheck is a function of the size of your income and the number of exemptions claimed. The higher your income and the fewer exemptions claimed, the more of your pay that will be withheld. Altering the number of exemptions you claim will have the effect of changing the amount withheld from your paycheck. If you claim more exemptions, your employer will withhold less each paycheck. Your goal should be to claim just enough exemptions for your employer to withhold your actual tax liability. If too much is withheld, you will be due a refund; if too little, you will be penalized by the IRS. If you have substantial amounts of unearned income (interest, dividends, and so forth), the problem is more complicated, because you will be required to make quarterly estimated tax payments.

Claim your aging relatives as exemptions when you provide over half of their financial support. Exemptions used in calculating your personal income tax liability are not limited to dependent children. You are also permitted to claim your parents or other relatives in the event that you provide over 50 percent of their financial support and they do not claim themselves on their own tax return. If you provide less than half their support because your brothers and sisters also help out, you and the participating members of your family are permitted to rotate the exemption, as long as you provide at least 10 percent of the support. If you intend to claim an exemption when you and others provide support for a relative, file IRS Form 2120.

Take advantage of the annual $10,000 gift tax exclusion. Your estate may be required to pay a federal estate tax if you have accumulated substantial assets during your life. Currently, unlimited assets can be left to a spouse, and up to $600,000 can be left to others, without your estate being required to pay federal estate taxes. Amounts above $600,000 left to nonspouses are taxed at stiff tax rates, and heirs have to pay inheritance taxes on much smaller amounts. You can reduce the taxes that would be levied on a large estate by utilizing the $10,000 annual gift tax exclusion. You are permitted to give away up to $10,000 annually to each of an unlimited number of individuals. These gifts are not taxable to you or to the recipients. The gifts meanwhile reduce the amount of the estate you will leave, as well as associated estate taxes, inheritance taxes, and attorney fees. Be aware that giving away assets that have appreciated in value (such as stocks) require the recipient to use your cost basis (the price you paid) in calculating taxes when the assets are sold. Thus, it is generally best to give cash. Appreciated property is a more appropriate gift to a charity.

Beware of leaving a large estate to a spouse. If you leave a large estate to your spouse, you will lose the potential benefits of the $600,000 estate and gift tax exclusion. Suppose you have accumulated $1.5 million in assets during your working years. You can leave everything to your spouse and thus avoid estate taxes. However, when your spouse subsequently dies and leaves the estate to your children, only $600,000 will be excluded from estate taxes; the remaining $900,000 will be taxed at relatively high rates. If instead you leave $900,000 to your spouse and the remaining $600,000 to your children, your estate will be free of estate taxes because of the unlimited exclusion for a spouse and the $600,000 exclusion to all other heirs. Now, when your spouse dies only $300,000 will be subject to estate taxes after the $600,000 exclusion, assuming your spouse's estate remains at $900,000. If your spouse remarries and leaves most of the estate to you-know-who, your children will be left out in the cold.

Don't forget to deduct expenses you incur for volunteer work. Certain tax deductions are permitted when you incur expenses as a volunteer for a charitable organization. If you use you vehicle for charitable work, you can to deduct 12 cents per mile (or the actual expense for gasoline), tolls, and parking fees you incur. (No deduction is permitted for depreciation or general repairs.) You can also deduct expenses for meals (at 50 percent of what you pay), transportation, and lodging, in the event that the charitable work involves an overnight or charity-sponsored meetings or conventions. You can also deduct out-of-pocket expenses for supplies, refreshments, and the purchase and care of uniforms. Maintain detailed records with receipts if you plan to utilize these deductions. Also keep in mind that you must itemize deductions (rather than take the standard deduction) in order to deduct charitable expenses or charitable contributions. You are not permitted to deduct the monetary value of the time you devote to charitable enterprises.

If you are married, think about filing separate federal tax returns. Married couples have for years been second-class citizens when it comes to paying federal taxes. You may be able to make a bad situation (your tax situation, not your marriage!) better by filing separate tax returns, one for your spouse and one for yourself. The bad news is that you will know if filing separately saves taxes only by preparing three returns; a joint return, your own return, and your spouse's return. Separate returns may result in substantial tax savings if you and your spouse are both employed and have substantially different amounts of deductible expenses. Medical deductions are valid only to the extent that they exceed 7.5 percent of your adjusted gross income. Casualty losses and miscellaneous deductions must exceed 10 percent and 2.5 percent of adjusted gross income, respectively. Filing separate returns may save taxes if either you or your spouse is more able to utilize the deductions. The deductions need only exceed the specified percentage of the adjusted gross income of the spouse with the majority of deductions, not of your joint income. If your income is relatively large, separate returns may also allow you to take greater advantage of your exemptions.

Don't forget to claim a tax deduction for seller-paid points on a mortgage loan. Individuals who purchase a principal residence can claim a federal income tax deduction for points paid to a lender, even if the points are paid by the seller of the property. Sellers sometimes agree to pay points (also called *loan origination fees*) on a loan in order to make the deal sweeter for the buyer and to close a sale, especially in a weak real estate market. The IRS treats seller-paid points as being paid to the buyer who, in turn, pays the points to the lender. This reduces the cost basis of the property by the amount of the seller-paid points.

Calculate your federal income tax liability. You should make a stab at calculating your federal income tax liability, even if you seek professional help to complete the tax return you will send to the Internal Revenue Service. By calculating your income taxes, you become familiar with the federal Tax Code, knowledge that will help you reduce your tax liability in subsequent years. You learn the difference between exemptions and deductions and understand the significance of your marginal tax rate. You also learn to identify deductible expenditures that can be used to reduce your tax liability.

AN OUTLINE FOR CALCULATING
YOUR FEDERAL INCOME TAX

	Wages
+	Interest and dividend income
+	Net capital gains
+	Other income
=	Gross income
−	Adjustments to income
=	Adjusted gross income
−	Standard deduction or itemized deductions
−	Exemptions
=	Taxable income
×	Tax rate(s)
=	Tax on taxable income
−	Tax credits
=	Tax liability

Only when you understand how your taxes are calculated can you be certain that you are providing your tax preparer with all the relevant information. Tax preparers sometimes make mistakes and omissions, so you may not be asked for every piece of information necessary to produce an accurate return. If you can't identify which expenses are allowed as deductions, you won't know which records to maintain. You may also find it interesting to compare your own calculations with those of the tax preparer. Tax forms are free from your local IRS and post office, and at many commercial banks and libraries. Inexpensive tax guides are available in most bookstores shortly after the first of the year.

Pay an annual IRA custodial fee by check and qualify for a deduction. If the custodian of your individual retirement account charges an annual maintenance fee (many brokerage firms and mutual funds charge annual fees that range from $10 to $50), you may be able to deduct the charge in calculating your federal income taxes, but only if you pay the fee with a separate check. You cannot claim the fee as a tax deduction if it is deducted directly from your IRA account. Keep in mind that you can only deduct from taxable income the investment-related and miscellaneous expenses that exceed 2 percent of your adjusted gross income (your gross income after certain specified adjustments). Paying your IRA fee by check will have no effect on your taxable income or your tax liability if you incur few other miscellaneous and investment-related expenses.

Wait until you are fifty-five or older to sell your principal residence. Homeowners fifty-five years of age and over are allowed a once-in-a-lifetime $125,000 exclusion on a gain from the sale of a residence. If you sell a residence at a gain prior to age fifty-five, you must either pay taxes on the gain or purchase another residence of equal or greater value, in which case you are permitted to defer the gain. If you or your spouse are nearing age fifty-five and considering the sale of your primary residence, you should probably delay the sale until one of you hits the magic birthday. Other rules apply in order to benefit from the exclusion: you must have owned and lived in the home for at least three years during the five years immediately preceding the date of sale. If you have been unlucky and lost money on your residences, no gain is realized and the age requirement is unimportant.

Claim medical expense deductions for improvements to your home, or special equipment installed in your home, when the main purpose is medical care. You are permitted to deduct expenses incurred for items such as entrance ramps, elevators, handrails, and widened doorways or hallways if these improvements are required for your medical care. These deductions are based on the difference between the cost you incur and the increase in the value of your home. For example, if you pay $1,700 to have entrance ramps installed at the front and back entrances, and an appraisal indicates the construction adds $300 to the value of your home, you are permitted a medical expense deduction of $1,400. You may deduct the total expense if the equipment or modification doesn't increase the value of your residence. Remember that medical expenses are deductible only to the extent that they exceed 7.5 percent of your adjusted gross income.

Don't overlook some of the most frequently overlooked medical deductions. Hospital and doctor bills that are not reimbursed by insurance are obvious medical expense deductions. Other expenses are not so obvious. You are permitted to deduct the expenses you incur for oxygen equipment, hearing aids, transportation essential for medical care, birth control pills, eyeglasses and contact lenses, a legal abortion, and expenses incurred as an organ donor. For more complete information concerning deductible medical expenses call the Internal Revenue Service at (800) 829–1040 and request Publication 502.

Time the payments you make for medical expenses. Because you are permitted to deduct medical expenses only to the extent that they exceed 7.5 percent of your adjusted gross income, it is difficult to use these expenses to reduce your tax liability. If you can bunch medical expenses in a particular year, you will increase the likelihood of pushing medical expenses above the 7.5 percent floor. If you know you will have insufficient medical expenses to utilize these deductions in the current year, push any subsequent payments for medical care into the next year. Pay bills late (after alerting the person you owe) or postpone certain voluntary treatments. In the last quarter of the year, consider putting off your physical exam, eye exam, or eyeglass purchase until after the first of the year. Deductions must be claimed in the year payments are made, not in the year of treatment.

Deduct a nonbusiness debt you are unable to collect. The Internal Revenue Service allows you to deduct a genuine nonbusiness debt in the year the debt becomes worthless. The debt must be genuine, and the entire amount of the debt must be uncollectible. Recovery of any collateral pledged against the loan reduces the amount of the deduction you are permitted. Provide careful documentation for the deduction, including a record of the steps you took to collect the debt and proof that the debtor disappeared, died, or declared bankruptcy. Any recovery that occurs subsequent to the deduction will have to be reported as income in the year of the recovery.

"Fingerprint" stock or mutual fund shares you sell to minimize tax consequences. If you purchase shares of a stock or mutual fund at different times and prices, you have a tax choice when you sell some of the shares. Suppose, for example, that you purchased 200 shares of XYZ for $40 each in January of 1990 and another 300 shares of the same firm for $60 each in February of 1992. If you decide to sell 200 of the total 500 shares at the current price of $70, are you selling shares with a cost basis of $40 or $60? The answer will have a major impact on the capital gains you report and the taxes you will be required to pay. Unless you specify otherwise, the IRS assumes the first shares sold are the first shares purchased (first in–first out). This method produces a capital gain of 200 x ($70–$40), or $6,000. However, if you instruct the broker to sell the most expensive shares and identify, or "fingerprint," those shares (by certificate number or by clear instruction), the capital gain is reduced to 200 x ($70–$60), or $2,000. Keep in mind that the burden of proof that you sold shares other than those purchased first rests on you.

If you file early and are due a refund, don't have it credited to next year's taxes. A return filed early in the year (January or early February) should result in a refund before the first estimated tax payment is due on April 15. Better that you have the money than the government. If you don't pay estimated taxes (taxes on income not subject to withholding), there is no reason to have the overpayment credited to next year's taxes. If you file late and make quarterly estimated payments, however, you won't get your hands on the refund check until after the first estimated tax payment is due to be paid. With a late filing and an estimated payment due, you will be better off to have the refund credited to next year's taxes (up to the amount of the first estimated tax payment).

Claim a tax credit for certain dependent care expenses. Taxpayers are permitted to claim a tax credit for certain dependent care expenses they incur while working or searching for work. Qualifying expenses include wages for household help (including relatives who are not dependents) and the cost of day care, summer day camp, and nursery school. The amount of the credit you can claim depends on the amount of your expenses and the amount of your adjusted gross income. The higher your adjusted gross income the lower the percentage of the expenses you are allowed as a credit. For example, if your adjusted gross income is over $28,000, you are permitted to claim only 20 percent of expenses up to a maximum of $2,400 (for a qualifying dependent) or $4,800 (for two or more qualifying dependents). You must complete IRS Form 2441 to claim the credit. For additional information, send for IRS publication 503 on child and dependent care expenses.

Arrange your marriage date according to your tax situation. If your future spouse is employed and earns an income similar to your own, it may pay to delay the marriage until after the first of the year. The tax penalty of being married can be significant—either filing jointly or filing separately and splitting the standard deduction—when you and your spouse have substantial amounts of earned income. If you delay the marriage until after the first of the year, you can file single returns for the current year. If, on the other hand, one of you earns substantially more income than the other, it may be to your economic benefit to marry prior to the end of the year so that you can take advantage of the lower tax rates for a joint return. Work through an estimate of the taxes you would pay filing a joint return and filing two single returns in order to determine the most financially advantageous time for marriage.

Arrange the date of your divorce or legal separation according to your tax situation. If you are certain of a divorce, it may be to your advantage to make the divorce or separation legal by the end of the year so that you and your soon-to-be ex-spouse can file single returns to escape the marriage penalty imposed on married couples. Filing single returns is especially advantageous when you each earn relatively high incomes. If one of you earns substantially more than the other, however, it may be better to divorce or separate next year so you can file a joint return for the current year.

Give securities that have appreciated in value to a family member who is in a lower tax bracket. Giving appreciated securities to another family member may result in lower taxes when the securities are sold, if the recipient pays taxes at a lower rate than you. The *amount* of any realized gain will remain unchanged because the securities will retain your cost basis. If you bought shares of stock at a price of $25 each, the recipient who sells the stock must show a cost basis of $25 per share even if the stock price was significantly higher than $25 at the time the gift was made. The potential tax advantage stems from the recipient's lower tax rate. In other words, the recipient of the gift will have the same amount of gain as if you had sold the shares, but the recipient's lower tax rate on the gain will result in a reduced tax liability. Of course, the strategy only makes sense if you are already planning to make a gift.

FREE IRS TAX PUBLICATIONS
OF INTEREST TO INVESTORS

The Internal Revenue Service provides an extensive list of free publications that are of interest to investors. The following publications can be obtained by calling (800) 829–3676 or by sending a request to one of the following forms distribution centers:

Western Area Distribution Center
Rancho Cordova, CA 95743

Eastern Area Distribution Center
P.O. Box 85074
Richmond, VA 23261

Central Area Distribution Center
P.O. Box 8903
Bloomington, IL 61702

Publication Number	Publication
526	*Charitable Contributions*
527	*Residential Rental Property*
544	*Sales and Other Dispositions of Assets*
550	*Investment Income and Expenses*
551	*Basis of Assets*
560	*Retirement Plans for the Self-Employed*
561	*Determining the Value of Donated Property*
564	*Mutual Fund Distributions*
571	*Tax-Sheltered Annuity Programs for Employees of Public Schools and Certain Tax-Exempt Organizations*
575	*Pension and Annuity Income*
590	*Individual Retirement Accounts*
909	*Alternative Minimum Tax for Individuals*
924	*Reporting of Real Estate Transactions to the IRS*
925	*Passive Activity and At-Risk Rules*
936	*Home Mortgage Interest Deduction*
1212	*List of Original Issue Discount Instruments*

Transfer income-producing assets to your children. Income earned by children under fourteen years of age is taxed at the same tax rate applied to income earned by the child's parents—after the first $1,200 of annual income earned by a child! The first $600 of annual investment income earned by children under fourteen years of age is tax-free. The next $600 of investment income is taxed at the child's rate, which is almost certainly lower than your tax rate. Take advantage of this section of the Tax Code by giving your child enough income-earning assets to earn $1,200 annually. A modest transfer of your investments reduces your tax liability without causing your child to pay much in taxes. To remain below the $1,200 limit (income earned each year will earn additional income in subsequent years), consider using each year's investment income to purchase Series EE U.S. savings bonds on which income taxes can be deferred until the child is at least fourteen years old. At fourteen, children are taxed separately and are likely to pay a relatively low tax rate on all their income. Keep in mind that money and investments must be irrevocably gifted to your child; you cannot later decide that you made a mistake and retrieve the assets you gave away.

Consider deferring income to next year. Most individual taxpayers operate on a cash basis, which means that most income is taxable only when the income is received. If you operate a business or have a sideline job, you may have some control over when income is received. Perhaps you provide personal consulting for a fee. Maybe you are a part-time writer who can request that payment for a manuscript be delayed for a period of time. Deferring income by a week or two so that it is received after the first of the year means you won't have to pay taxes on the income for another year. Whether you will benefit from this tactic depends on your probable tax rate for next year's income compared to the top tax rate you will pay on this year's income. A lower tax rate next year makes it more beneficial to defer income.

Give it away, don't throw it away. Most things you own have value to someone, even though they may not have value to you. You may replace your current, working coffeemaker with one that is bigger, fancier, or better looking. You may buy new porch furniture because you want a "new look" or more comfortable chairs. You are likely to replace clothing before it is worn out. Your tax liability can be reduced by giving replaced or unwanted items to charitable organizations rather than throwing them away. You are allowed to deduct the fair market value (the price an item would bring from a sale) of property donated to charitable organizations in calculating your income tax liability. You must obtain a receipt that indicates the items donated along with their current market values. Property donations of over $250 require a professional evaluation. Note that charitable donations reduce your tax liability only in years when you choose to itemize deductions rather than claim the standard deduction.

Use the long form. The Internal Revenue Service allows you to compute your federal income tax liability using either a short form or a long form. The short form is easier to complete, but may cause you to miss deductions or adjustments you are entitled to claim. The long form takes more time, but it calls your attention to deductions and adjustments you might otherwise miss.

Complete your tax returns as early as possible. If you are entitled to a refund, the sooner your return is completed and filed, the sooner you will receive the refund. On the other hand, if the return indicates that you owe additional taxes (*i.e.,* your total tax liability exceeds the sum of your withholding and estimated tax payments), you can wait to file the return on the last possible date, generally April 15. Don't assume that you know your tax liability, either for better or worse. You can't know for certain until the return is actually completed. Complete the calculations early just in case the federal or state government owes you money. You don't have anything to lose.

Make financial decisions based on your marginal tax rate. Many financial calculations require that you use your marginal tax rate. The marginal tax rate is the tax you pay on each additional dollar of taxable income. For example, if a $100 raise causes you to pay an additional $28 in income taxes, your marginal tax rate is $28/$100, or 28 percent. Your marginal tax rate indicates the amount you will save in taxes by making a charitable deduction or a tax-deductible purchase. Knowing your marginal tax rate also allows you to make a an informed decision between investing in a tax-exempt municipal bond and a taxable corporate bond. Understanding your marginal tax rate helps you to determine whether you will gain by working overtime or taking a second job. To determine your marginal tax rate, look at last year's tax return and calculate the additional tax you would have paid with an extra $100 of taxable income.

Request that your employer reimburse your travel expenses rather than add the amounts to income. Suppose you incur

$250 of travel expenses related to your employment, and your employer chooses to reimburse you by adding $250 to your regular income. Although the extra $250 will be reported as regular income subject to federal and state taxes, the travel expenses you incurred are allowed as a deduction, thus canceling out the additional income. Maybe. Being reimbursed for travel expenses with an increase in income works fine as long as sufficient other miscellaneous deductions are available to meet the 2 percent (of adjusted gross income) minimum established by the federal government. You are only permitted to deduct from adjusted gross income the miscellaneous deductions that *exceed* 2 percent of this income; you may find that the travel expenses you incur cannot be deducted. It is best for you to receive direct reimbursement for expenses you incur.

If you estimate that your taxes are being underpaid, ask your employer to increase your withholding. You will be penalized by the Internal Revenue Service if your withholding and estimated taxes are less than 90 percent of your income tax liability for the year. A penalty is most often assessed because you have income, such as dividends and interest, that is not subject to withholding by an employer. Several months prior to the end of the tax year, estimate the taxes you will owe for the year and compare this amount with your projected withholding and estimated taxes for the year. If your estimate indicates that you will owe a substantial additional amount of taxes on April 15, request that your employer increase the amount withheld from your last few paychecks of the year. Closing the gap with increased withholding even at the end of the year, will allow you to avoid a penalty.

Use a credit card to charge charitable donations. Charitable contributions are tax-deductible regardless of whether you contribute with cash, check, or on your credit card. If the end of the year is fast approaching and funds are temporarily unavailable for a planned donation, think about charging the donation on your credit card. You can deduct the donation in the year it is charged, even though the charge will appear on your statement and be paid in the following year. If you choose the right credit card, you will also benefit from additional frequent flier points or a rebate. On the negative side, the charity will not receive the entire amount of the charge because of the service fee deducted by the card issuer. Keep in mind, as well, that some charities are not set up to accept donations via charge cards.

CHAPTER 9

Transportation Money Smarts

Consider maintenance expenses, insurance premiums, and resale value when you choose a vehicle. Smaller vehicles generally cost less to buy and less to own. Intelligent driving habits save on maintenance and energy costs. Using public transportation in place of your own vehicle can save a bundle. It is sometimes wise to cancel collision and comprehensive insurance coverage for older vehicles.

Beware of mechanical devices that promise gas savings for your automobiles. Most gas-saving devices are much like the fountain of youth—they sound good but don't live up to their promise. The Environmental Protection Agency found that of over 100 alleged gas-saving devices it tested, only a few produced even a tiny savings. The moral: skip the mystery devices, and use the money you save to pay for a tune-up.

Take your own oil and filter when you have your vehicle's oil changed. Most auto service facilities that offer oil and filter changes will deduct the cost of filters and oil that you supply. For example, a service station advertising an $18.95 oil and filter change may be willing to deduct $1.50 per quart of oil that you supply and an additional $2.99, if you supply the filter. A careful reader of newspaper advertisements can generally purchase oil and filters on sale at prices below those charged by auto service centers. Ask someone at the service station to which you plan to take your car *before* you try this. You can save even more money by changing the oil and filter yourself.

Gas up your vehicle before the tank is nearly empty. Waiting to stop for gas until your vehicle is operating on fumes reduces your flexibility; you have to purchase gasoline from the nearest station, and thereby increase the likelihood of paying a high price for fuel. Start thinking about filling the vehicle's tank when the fuel gauge indicator hits the half-full mark, when you still have time to do some serious price shopping. This tip works just as well for cross-country as for local driving. Make it a rule to occasionally check the gas gauge. If you slip up and have to buy fuel in a hurry, don't fill the tank if you feel the price is too high. Buy enough gasoline to last until you can locate a station with a more competitive price.

Employ the services of a travel agency that rebates a portion of your travel expenses. Rebates of 5 percent are available for transportation and lodging expenses incurred, when you book reservations through particular travel services. You may qualify for these benefits by holding certain credit cards or memberships. A fee is sometimes charged for membership but can in some cases be waived. The travel services that pay rebates actually share a portion of the fees they receive from the airlines, cruise lines, and hotels on which they book travel. These services are best suited for individuals who plan their own itinerary, although the travel services will usually assist in locating the best prices for airline tickets and hotel rooms. Rebates are obtained by submitting receipts for transportation and lodging expenses *after* travel has occurred. In other words, the rebate is a partial refund of your expenses, not an advance. A number of organizations, including several banks, offer travel services or the opportunity to become a member of a travel service to their customers.

Drive your old car a few years longer. The decline in the market value, or depreciation, of a vehicle is a major expense of ownership. Depending on the age of your vehicle and the number of miles you generally drive each year, depreciation may be the single largest expense of owning your automobile. Annual depreciation is largest when a vehicle is relatively new and generally declines each year as the vehicle ages. A vehicle five to six years old has already absorbed most of its depreciation and will decline relatively little in value in subsequent years. Because older vehicles depreciate little, an owner can afford to put substantial amounts into maintenance to keep the vehicles operating and still come out ahead, because he or she defers the purchase of another vehicle. When you consider the financing, insurance, and taxes on a newer vehicle, the comparison is even more striking. Trading for a newer vehicle is easier to justify if dependable transportation is a very important consideration.

Don't lease if you normally keep a vehicle for over five years. If you trade for a new vehicle every two of three years, a lease may be your best bet. Leasing is likely to be an expensive financing option, however, if you generally keep a vehicle for many years. Car dealers advertise low lease payments to sell cars, but most popular leases allow the dealer to retain ownership of the vehicle at the end of the lease. You then must purchase the leased car or purchase or lease a different car. The lease payment will be lower than the corresponding loan payment over the same time period as the lease (twenty-four months, thirty-six months, and so forth), but you are left without wheels at the end of the lease. On the other hand, you are the owner of a vehicle when you make the final payment on the loan. A lease is a particularly bad deal when you expect to put relatively few miles on a vehicle. The fewer miles you drive, the longer the vehicle should last, and the more advantageous it is to purchase.

Read the fine print before you lease a vehicle. Leasing a vehicle may look like a bargain, but it is wise to check the fine print. You will almost certainly be hit with extra charges if you drive more than a specified number of miles. Most leasing firms allow an average of up to 15,000 miles per year without penalty. You may be required to pay an additional 15 cents per mile or more for every mile you drive over 30,000 miles on a two-year lease or 45,000 miles on a three-year lease. The fine print may also specify that you pay a $2,000 or $3,000 nonrefundable deposit in order to qualify for the lease. Factoring in the initial cash payment required to qualify for an advertised lease may add up to a much higher cost.

Purchase a small vehicle. Compared to highway Goliaths, small automobiles are nearly always less expensive to buy, operate, and insure, and return a larger proportion of your initial outlay at trade-in time. Small vehicles also consume less space in your garage, enabling you to accumulate more junk. Small vehicles get better gas mileage, hold less oil and anti-freeze, use smaller and less expensive tires, and are easier to push start. Of course, initial cost and the expense of operating a vehicle are not the only considerations when choosing a vehicle to own. A small car may not meet your needs if you have a large family, despite the savings you will enjoy. In the event of an automobile accident, you are more likely to suffer injuries in a small vehicle. Most small vehicles are also less comfortable for long-distance traveling.

If you are unable to obtain a discounted airline seat, keep trying. If you just telephoned about an airline reservation and were told that the cheap seats were all gone, don't give up. Airlines limit discounted seats on each flight, mostly on the basis of the number of seats they expect to sell at full price. Why should they sell a ticket at a discounted price when the seat is expected to bring full price before the de-

PAYMENTS AND FINANCE CHARGES FOR
AUTOMOBILE LOANS OF DIFFERENT LENGTHS

Loan length	3 years	4 years	5 years
Amount borrowed	$17,000	$17,000	$17,000
Interest rate	8%	8%	8%
Monthly payment	$532.72	$415.02	$344.70
Total payments	$19,177.92	$19,920.96	$20,682.00
Total interest paid	$2,177.92	$2,920.96	$3,682.00

parture date? Airlines typically issue more discounted tickets on flights that are not expected to fill, while flights that are normally full will have few bargain seats. Airlines constantly fiddle with the mix of full-fare and discounted seats for each flight in order to produce the maximum revenue. If a flight isn't filling as rapidly as expected, airline management might open additional discount seats. Thus, if you call one day and find no discounted seats are available, don't give up. Keep calling; additional cheap seats may become available, or someone who has a reservation at a discounted price may cancel, leaving their vacated seat available.

Join a travel club if you do a lot of traveling. Several organizations offer travel club memberships that allow you to book hotels at half price. These memberships also sometimes provide discounts at restaurants and attractions. Memberships ordinarily entail an annual fee, although you may qualify for free membership if you hold certain credit cards, belong to particular organizations, or do business with companies that offer free membership as a benefit.

Most listed hotels offer half-price rooms on a space-available basis, which means that you will sometimes be unable to book a room at half price. The discount is generally based on the full price (called the *rack rate*) of a hotel's more expensive rooms (one with a view, for example). Thus, you are unlikely to obtain a real discount of 50 percent for the room you would be most likely to rent. Still, these memberships often provide good value and can be a real benefit if you travel frequently. A few clubs also offer discounts for travel abroad. Entertainment Publishing (800–285–5525) sells the *National Hotel Directory* ($27.95) offering discounts on U.S. hotels, and the *Entertainment Europe Book* ($43) with discounts on European hotels.

Choose a low-maintenance vehicle. The initial cost of a vehicle is so imposing that it may overshadow other important financial considerations, such as financing and maintenance. It is a serious mistake to disregard maintenance expense when choosing a new or used vehicle. Saving four or five hundred dollars in initial outlay while purchasing a high-maintenance vehicle is false savings. Maintenance expense is a function both of reliability and the cost of repairs. You can always end up with a lemon, of course, but certain vehicles have a history of requiring frequent maintenance and/or expensive repairs. For example, certain foreign-made vehicles have a history of reliability, but when something goes wrong you pay the piper. *Consumer Reports'* annual automotive edition and year-end special edition each provide information on vehicle reliability. The publication even recommends which models to buy and which to avoid. When buying a new vehicle, assume that history is a relatively accurate guide to the future. That is, if a particular model vehicle has a poor reliability record, it is a good bet that the current model will suffer the same problems.

Always attempt to negotiate a lower rate for a hotel room. When you make a hotel reservation, don't assume that the price you are quoted is the lowest price available. Unless the hotel management expects the hotel to be full during the period of your stay, the rate will probably be negotiable. Ask if the hotel gives discounts for business travelers, seniors, American Automobile Association members, or any other organization in which you can claim membership. If the hotel is part of a chain or association, you will be more successful at negotiating a favorable rate by phoning the hotel directly. Central reservation services usually cannot negotiate room rates. Try to negotiate a lower rate at the reservation desk as well. This is most effective if you don't already have a reservation. However, even if you do have a reservation at a previously quoted price, you should ask about the lowest available room rate *before informing the clerk that you have a reservation*. If the newly quoted rate is lower than the rate for your reservation ask for the new rate.

Shop hard for the best rate on a rental car. The rental car business is competitive, and you should call at least four or five companies for prices before your choose a rental vehicle. Check with some of the smaller firms as well as the large national companies. Don't forget to inquire about the cost of insurance waivers, returning a car without a full tank of gas, and mileage charges when you compare firms. Also ask about the discounts that are often granted to members of AAA, AARP, frequent flier programs, and others. Each program may result in a different discount. Make a list of the discounts for which you qualify *before* calling. Shopping is particularly important when you will be using a one-way rental. Some rental companies charge a drop-off fee that can exceed the rental fee. Other firms have no drop-off surcharge but levy a higher mileage charge. Substantial differences in pricing can produce real savings if you are a careful shopper.

Check with an airline ticket consolidator before you purchase an airline ticket. Ticket consolidators make bulk purchases of airline tickets, which they then offer to travel agents and individuals. Consolidators negotiate steep discounts that they are able to pass along in lower ticket prices to individuals. They offer particularly attractive prices when you need a ticket too quickly to qualify for the airlines' restrictions on advance purchase. Consolidators can also save you money on peak-season flights, when discount tickets are difficult to obtain. Beware of any special restrictions on tickets purchased from a consolidator, and check out the reputation of any firm with which you haven't previously done business. Don't buy from a consolidator until you have checked with an airline on the price of a comparable ticket. What seems a good deal sometimes isn't.

Know the amount a dealer pays for a new vehicle before you go shopping for a new car or truck. Knowing how much someone paid for something is a big plus when you go shopping. If only one seller is available, this knowledge may not help a great deal because you have no other sources. But when numerous sellers offer an identical item, as with a new vehicle, knowledge of the sellers' cost will give you a good idea of where to begin the bargaining. Several inexpensive paperback books (available in the magazine section of most bookstores) provide information on dealer cost and the retail price for most new vehicles and available options. Or contact *Consumer Reports* (800–933–5555) and request a quotation by phone, fax, or mail. The cost is $11, $20, and $27 for one, two, and three reports, respectively. This information is an inexpensive investment that may save hundreds or even thousands of dollars.

Negotiate the rate on a rental car. Do some last-minute shopping at the airport if you will be picking up an airport rental car, *even if you already have a reservation.* Rental firms with excess inventory (maybe some people with reservations didn't show) will sometimes be willing to deal, and you can obtain a lower price than you were quoted on the telephone at the time the reservation was made. Indicate the price quotation for your reservation to encourage another rental company to beat the price or offer a bigger or better vehicle at the same price. If you already have a reservation with a confirmed price, you have nothing to lose and everything to gain by seeking to better your situation. It's the American way.

Don't assume that a travel agent will always obtain the lowest price for a ticket or reservation. Travel agents claim they have access to huge data banks of up-to-date information, allowing them to obtain the lowest available prices for airline tickets, auto rentals, hotels, and so forth. Don't believe it! Travel agents *may* be able to obtain low prices, but not necessarily the lowest prices. Do some investigating on your own before you call a travel agent. After the agent quotes a price, make a few more calls to determine whether you have received the best possible deal. If you uncover a lower price, call the travel agent back and request the better deal. Prices for airline tickets and hotel rooms are constantly changing and you can sometimes obtain substantial savings by doing your own shopping.

Wait until the end of the model year before purchasing a new vehicle. You can nearly always obtain the lowest price on a new vehicle at the end of the model year. If you typically drive a vehicle for eight to ten years, the market value of the car when you're ready to trade won't be much different if the car is one year older. In other words, in 2004 it will hardly matter whether the car you are trading or selling is a 1996 model or a 1997 model. You will pay a substantially different price, however, to purchase an end-of-year 1996 model compared to a beginning-of-year 1997 model. Manufacturers sometimes offer car dealers thousands of dollars of incentives on vehicles that the dealers are holding at the end of a model year. You may be able to purchase a vehicle for less than the invoice cost to the dealer.

Use carpet samples as vehicle floor mats. Auto floor mats can be one of America's biggest rip-offs. Floor mats from an automobile dealer often cost $60, $80, or even $100 a pair. Floor mats from a discount store or automobile supply store will be less expensive, but still cost up to $40 for mats of medium quality. How about some high quality mats for $2 or $3 each? Next time you need a new set of floor mats, try carpet or furniture stores that sell carpet. These stores often dispose of samples of discontinued carpets for $2 to $3 each. You will find thick pile carpet that would cost a bundle if it came on regular floor mats and other types of carpet that may be more appropriate for the use you give your vehicle. You will also have a wide choice of colors. Call ahead so you don't end up driving to a carpet store with no samples for sale.

Do your homework before shopping for a used vehicle. You can only be a wise shopper by knowing at what price something can be purchased. This knowledge is especially important when you are planning to buy something expensive, such a used vehicle. Scour the classified sections in several newspapers before you begin shopping to find out how much sellers are asking for the type of vehicle you are interested in purchasing. Call your bank or credit union and ask about the loan value and wholesale price for the vehicle. The wholesale price represents approximately how much the seller could obtain in a trade or by selling the vehicle to a dealer. If you locate a vehicle being sold for less than wholesale, you are either getting a very good deal or a very bad vehicle. Knowledge is power, especially in shopping.

Offer a car dealer his cost for a new vehicle. Instead of offering a fair price for a new vehicle and then negotiating upward, initially offer a low price and see what develops. Start with dealer cost, which you can obtain from magazines in most bookstores or from one of several services that provide this information. Although you probably won't be able to purchase the vehicle at cost, you may obtain a price ranging from $300 to $500 above cost, which is fair for both you and the dealer.

Check airline fares in nearby cities. Just because it costs $460 roundtrip to fly from your local airport to a particular city doesn't mean the cost of the trip is necessarily the same from a nearby airport. Airlines frequently offer special fares in and out of certain locations to be more competitive, offer new service, or drum up additional traffic. For example, residents of Atlanta can sometimes save a bundle by driving to Birmingham, Alabama. Likewise, you may be able to save on a ticket by driving from Tampa to Orlando (or vice versa). Discounted seats are often available on flights from some airports but not from other airports. Your potential savings are particularly great if your local airport is served by a single airline; lack of competition usually results in high ticket prices. This doesn't mean you should drive an extra 300 miles in order to save $30 on an airline ticket. Depending on where you live, however, you may be able to drive 100 miles and save several hundred dollars. You are the one who must decide whether the added hassle of the drive is worth the savings. Everything in life is a trade-off.

Don't purchase gasoline with an octane higher than your vehicle requires. Super premium gasoline will not make your vehicle go like a rocket or turn your ordinary sedan into a powerful sports car. Buying gasoline with a higher octane than your vehicle requires is as useful as flushing money down the toilet. Typically, it costs an extra 10 cents for each grade level you upgrade. Thus, super premium gasoline will cost from 20 to 25 cents per gallon more than regular unleaded. Determine the octane your engine requires by reading the owner's manual. If you can't locate the manual, or you have the manual but can't find the information, call the dealer. The octane of a gasoline will be posted on the pump. Select the grade with the lowest octane sufficient to meet the minimum requirement for your vehicle, fill the tank, and save $3 to $5.

MONTHLY SAVINGS REQUIRED TO ACCUMULATE $17,000			
	Savings Period		
Return on Savings	36 Months	48 Months	60 Months
5 percent	$438.67	$320.66	$249.98
6 percent	432.17	314.25	243.66
7 percent	425.74	307.92	237.45
8 percent	419.39	301.69	231.37
9 percent	413.10	295.55	225.39
10 percent	406.88	289.50	219.53

Ask for compensation if your airline flight is canceled or delayed. Airlines are not required to provide compensation in the event your flight is delayed or canceled by mechanical problems or nasty weather. You are legally entitled to a seat on the next available flight to your destination. Buuuuutttt . . . if you inquire at the check-in counter, the airline may be willing to provide you with a voucher for a meal and, if you are delayed overnight, a hotel. You don't have to make a fuss. Merely ask if the airline compensates passengers on delayed flights. The longer your delay, the more likely the airline will agree to provide compensation. Although airlines rarely announce any offer of compensation at the terminal, attendants want to maintain good relations with customers, especially customers who are frequent travelers; airlines would rather spend a few dollars now than lose your loyalty and future bookings.

Stop at welcome centers when you are traveling. State and city welcome stations not only provide a place to rest, they also often prove to be a terrific source of discount coupons for motels, hotels, campgrounds, restaurants, and attractions that are located down the highway. It is not unusual to find a coupon that offers a motel room for $10 to $15 less than the price you would otherwise be charged. A coupon may allow a family to stay overnight for the same room rate as an individual. You may learn of a nearby bed and breakfast that would provide a welcome change to yet another faceless motel. Employees at many welcome centers will phone ahead to a particular motel to determine whether rooms are available at the special rate.

Charge rental cars on a credit card that provides free insurance coverage. Buying collision and comprehensive insurance through auto rental companies is very expensive. To determine if your credit card includes rental insurance, read the agreement from the issuer or call the telephone number listed on the card, and ask. American Express cards provide rental coverage for most types of rentals as do gold VISA cards. Understand that coverage from the card company is generally secondary to coverage on your personal insurance policy. Thus, if your personal auto insur- ance includes coverage for rental vehicles, the card issuer will reimburse you for a loss only to the extent that the loss is not fully paid by your insurer. Check on any types of vehicles or driving that may be excluded. Trucks, large vans, luxury vehicles, and motor homes are often not covered.

Use a rental vehicle when you plan to drive a long distance in a short time. The cost of operating a relatively new vehicle is so high that it can pay you to rent a car if you plan a lengthy trip in a short period of time. Suppose you have a need to drive 250 miles to a city on business and would like to return on the same day. The 500-mile drive would result in significant wear and tear on your vehicle. Figure the expense of wear on your vehicle at a rate at least 20 to 25 cents per mile *exclusive of fuel*. This cost includes the wear of tires and mechanical parts, being closer to needing another oil and filter change, and so forth. Even at the low end of the estimate you are talking about transportation costs of at least $100. Now consider that you can sometimes rent a vehicle with unlimited mileage for $25 to $40 per day. You pay for the gas, of course, but you would incur the same expense for your own vehicle. The comparison is less favorable if you will be required to stay overnight or will be driving a relatively short distance.

Shop around if you intend to purchase an extended warranty for a new or used vehicle. Automobile dealers are not the only source for extended vehicle warranties. For example, American Automobile Association members can purchase extended warranties on new and used vehicles through AAA. Likewise, individuals who carry auto insurance through GEICO can purchase extended warranties on their insured vehicles. You can't always save money by purchasing an extended warranty from someone other than a dealer, but you *may* save money by shopping elsewhere. Vehicle buyers are generally allowed a period of time after purchasing a vehicle to decide if they wish to buy an extended warranty through the dealer. Use the time wisely; shop for a comparable warranty elsewhere at a better price. Of course, you may prefer to avoid purchasing an extended warranty from any source.

Obtain an independent inspection before purchasing a used vehicle. An automobile, truck, or van will almost surely be one of your most expensive purchases, even if the vehicle was previously owned. At the same time, mechanical problems with used vehicles, even recently acquired vehicles, are a common consumer complaint. One method for reducing the likelihood of expensive repairs is to have an independent inspection of a used vehicle you are thinking of purchasing. It is unrealistic to expect that the seller has corrected all known defects. It is equally unrealistic to expect the seller, who is trying to make a sale, to reveal every flaw. Problems may exist that the seller doesn't know about. A thorough inspection prior to purchasing a used vehicle is always worthwhile, especially if no warranty is included. If you aren't comfortable conducting your own inspection, take the vehicle to a trusty mechanic or to a business that will perform an inspection for a fee. Paying $50 to $100 to uncover potential problems may save hundreds or even thousands of dollars in repair expenses. Remember, used vehicle purchases are made with buyer beware. The more expensive the vehicle you expect to purchase, the more value you get for the cost of an inspection. You need someone on your side who is able to evaluate the quality of the product you are thinking about purchasing.

Check on senior airline tickets. The major airlines offer bargain-priced ticket vouchers for seniors who frequently travel long-distance. Typically, the vouchers must be purchased in books of four or eight. In 1995, a book of four vouchers cost approximately $600, or $150 each. A book of eight vouchers cost approximately $1,000, or $125 each. Restrictions vary somewhat by airline, but most airlines allow you to use a voucher as full payment for a ticket to any destination within the continental U.S. or Canada. A second ticket is required for the return flight. Thus, buying an eight-voucher pack allows you to fly from coast to coast and return for two vouchers that cost about $250, a real bargain on a long-distance flight. Senior vouchers entail some restrictions. You must be at least sixty-two years old to qualify. Vouchers generally expire one year from the date of purchase and cannot be transferred (your traveling companion must qualify and buy his or her own ticket vouchers). You must make a reservation at least fourteen days prior to the date on which you wish to travel or agree to fly standby.

Maintain proper air pressure in your vehicle's tires. Most vehicle owners, probably including yourself, seldom check tire air pressure unless a tire appears nearly flat. Many vehicles roll on down the highways with low tire air pressure, which increases rolling resistance and reduces the gas mileage of any vehicle. Maintaining correct air pressure can improve the mileage of your vehicle by up to 5 percent and produce significant savings during a year of driving. The degree to which mileage is reduced depends on several factors, including the type of tire used, the speed at which you normally drive, and the difference between the recommended and actual tire pressure. To make checking air pressure as easy as possible, invest a few dollars in a good quality tire pressure gauge, which can be purchased at most discount or auto supply stores. This investment will pay for itself many times. Proper tire inflation also lengthens the life of your tires, thereby producing additional savings.

Determine the total cost of a set of tires before you purchase the tires. You probably discovered when you purchased your last set of tires that the price you paid was significantly higher than the advertised price. After the retailer added balancing, new stems, a road hazard warranty, (all of which were optional) and the sales tax, you may have paid 30 to 40 percent more than the advertised price. There isn't much you can do about the sales tax, of course, but you should check on any additional expenses *before* you purchase a set of tires. Most tire dealers include mounting, and some include balancing, in the quoted price. Determine exactly what you plan to purchase (new stems, balancing, or whatever) and request a bottom-line price for the entire purchase. This is the only way you can compare prices among dealers. Consider having the tires balanced somewhere other than at the dealer where you purchase the tires, since auto service centers periodically offer specials on balancing.

Don't purchase expensive tires for a car you soon plan to trade. If you plan to trade your car within the next year or so, you are wasting your money to purchase expensive tires that have a long mileage warranty. Why pay a lot of money for tires with a 50,000 mileage warranty when you expect to drive the vehicle no more than 10,000 miles before trading for another vehicle? You are saving money for the next owner of your vehicle, not for yourself. If you need new tires, consider the mileage you are likely to put on the vehicle before trading. While you don't want to purchase tires that will wear out prior to trading the vehicle, you also don't want to squander your money on something you aren't likely to use.

Wash your vehicle yourself. Washing your own vehicle is an easy way to save money while assuring yourself that the job is done correctly. You are the one who chooses the soap, sponge, and chamois or towel. You can make certain the items used to clean the vehicle are up to your requirements and meet the standards recommended by the vehicle's manufacturer. Why pay $5.95 to $7.95 for a part-mechanical, part-human commercial wash, when you can wash the vehicle yourself for almost nothing?

Sell your vehicle yourself. Although it is a lot easier to trade in your current vehicle when you are in the market for a new automobile or truck, choosing the trade route is likely to cost you hundreds or even thousands of dollars compared to what you would get by selling the vehicle yourself. Dealers will usually pay you no more than the wholesale value for your old vehicle. In fact, the initial offer from the dealer may be lower than wholesale. Selling the vehicle yourself will allow you to negotiate a price for the new vehicle without obscuring what you are actually paying. Check dealer and classified advertisements and nearby used car lots to determine the price that vehicles similar to yours are bringing. Paperback books available at most magazine stands also provide used car values, but the information is sometimes dated and may not reflect vehicle prices in your particular region. Spend some effort to make your vehicle visually appealing to potential buyers. Be realistic regarding a price and include the price in your advertisements.

Drive conservatively. Aggressive driving costs money. Fast starts, rapid acceleration, sudden stops, and speeding all consume extra fuel, burn more rubber, and wear down the brake pads. Poor driving habits result in otherwise avoidable accidents that drive up insurance rates and depreciate your vehicle. Conservative driving practices, on the other hand, will better preserve the value of your vehicle as well as substantially reduce the money you spend for fuel and maintenance. Driving as if an egg is on the accelerator pedal can make the bacon you bring home go a lot farther.

Buy two airline tickets for less than the cost of one ticket. Airlines often require a Saturday stay in order to qualify for the lowest fare. A round-trip ticket that includes a Saturday at your destination may cost $375, while a round-trip ticket without a Saturday stay may cost more than twice as much. If you can't spend a Saturday, the solution is simple; purchase two round-trip tickets, each with a Saturday layover, but originating at different locations. Suppose you need to fly from Tallahassee to Los Angeles for two days of midweek business meetings and can't bear the thought of lengthening the stay to include a weekend. If the price of a round-trip ticket without a Saturday stay knocks your socks off, buy one round-trip ticket that originates in Tallahassee on the day you want to depart, with the return on any day that qualifies for the lowest fare. The return date on this round-trip ticket doesn't matter because you won't be using it. Now order a second round-trip ticket that originates in Los Angeles on the day you wish to return and accept whatever return date is cheapest, because you won't be using the second half of this ticket either. Now you are set. Use the first half of the Tallahassee–L.A.–Tallahassee ticket and the first half of the L.A.–Tallahassee–L.A. ticket for the return.

Rid yourself of extra vehicles. You probably know some

families with more vehicles than family members who are licensed to drive. If this applies to your family, you can reduce your expenses by selling, donating, or junking the extra vehicle(s). A vehicle can be viewed as an investment that earns a negative return, and the fewer of these you own the better. Even older vehicles with little market value require outlays for insurance, tags, and maintenance. Owning an extra vehicle that is relatively new only increases the expenses. Don't underestimate the extra expenses of owning a pickup truck that you drive only on the weekends. Maintain a record of the amounts being spent on the vehicles you own to determine how much money you would save by getting rid of one of them.

Walk or ride a bicycle in place of driving. Next time you visit a nearby friend, do both your health and your billfold a favor by choosing to walk or ride a bicycle instead of drive. Why spend money to exercise at the YMCA, when you can walk or ride your bicycle for free? Perhaps it is possible to walk or ride a bike to the store or even to work. Every time your vehicle is left in the garage you will be leaving dollars in your pocket. Avoiding short driving trips should also extend the life of your vehicle, since this type of driving causes above-average wear and tear on the vehicle's moving parts. Your ability to sensibly substitute pedal power for horse power depends on where you live, of course.

Have your children who are college students leave their vehicles at home. The expense of a college education can be substantially reduced when vehicles remain at home. Most college campuses and campus activities are designed so that students can function perfectly well without owning a vehicle. If a campus is large or time between classes is short, a bicycle or public transportation will fill the bill. Most college campuses lack adequate parking, which makes having a vehicle a real headache anyway. Without a vehicle at college, your student will also tend to find things to do on campus, not a bad consequence.

Use alternate airport parking. Airports now treat parking facilities as major profit centers, overcharging you to leave your vehicle in the airport parking lot when you fly. You can avoid parking fees by having someone drop you off or by choosing to take public transportation to the airport, but you must live in relatively close proximity to make this option viable. If you must drive your own vehicle to the airport, consider alternate parking facilities. For example, some rental car companies permit you to park your vehicle in their lot for less than the airport charges. You may save from $1.50 to $2.50 per day using this option. You can also leave your vehicle at a nearby hotel or motel. Management is more likely to allow you to leave your vehicle if you plan to stay overnight the night before or the night after your planned trip. You will want to choose a hotel or motel that offers a shuttle service to the airport. Nearly all car rental companies offer shuttle service.

Index

Warranties
   credit card purchases,
      with, 18
   cost and value, 89–90,
      194
Welcome centers, 193
Wiring funds, 129

Y

Yellow Pages, 5, 27

About the Author

David L. Scott is Professor of Accounting and Finance at Valdosta State University, Valdosta, Georgia. He was born in Rushville, Indiana, and received degrees from Purdue University and Florida State University before earning a Ph.D. in economics at the University of Arkansas at Fayetteville.

Professor Scott has written two dozen books on personal finance and investing, including eight other volumes in the *Money Smarts* series, *How Wall Street Works* (Irwin Professional Publishing), and *Wall Street Words* (Houghton Mifflin). He regularly conducts workshops on topics related to investing and personal finance.

Dr. Scott and his wife, Kay, are the authors of the two-volume *Guide to the National Park Areas,* published by the Globe Pequot Press. They spend their summers traveling throughout the United States and Canada in their fourth Volkswagen camper.

Globe Pequot Business Books

If you have found *The Guide to Saving Money* informative, please be sure to read the following Globe Pequot business books.

Money Smarts Series

The Guide to Personal Budgeting
How to Stretch Your Dollars Through Wise Money Management, $9.95
by David L. Scott

The Guide to Investing in Common Stocks
How to Build Your Wealth by Mastering the Basic Strategies, $9.95
by David L. Scott

The Guide to Investing in Bonds
How to Build Your Wealth by Mastering the Basic Strategies, $9.95
by David L. Scott

The Guide to Investing in Mutual Funds
How to Build Your Wealth by Mastering the Basic Strategies, $9.95
by David L. Scott

The Guide to Buying Insurance
How to Secure the Coverage You Need at An Affordable Price, $9.95
by David L. Scott

The Guide to Managing Credit
How to Stretch Your Dollars Through Wise Credit Management, $9.95
by David L. Scott

The Guide to Tax-Saving Investing
How to Build Your Wealth by Mastering the Basic Strategies, $9.95
by David L. Scott

The Guide to Investing for Current Income
How to Build Your Wealth by Mastering the Basic Strategies, $9.95
by David L. Scott

For beginning investors we suggest
Learning to Invest
A Beginner's Guide to Building Personal Wealth, $9.95
by Beatson Wallace

To order any of these titles with MASTERCARD or VISA, call toll-free (800) 243–0495. Free shipping on three or more books ordered. Connecticut residents add sales tax. Please request a catalogue of other quality Globe Pequot titles, which include books on travel, outdoor recreation, nature, gardening, cooking, nature, and more. Prices and availability subject to change.